Past and Present

The Cotswold Line

Past and Present

Subscribers' Limited Edition

Published to mark the completion of the
Cotswold line redoubling project.

Subscribers' Edition limited to 400 copies

....

John Stretton

....

Tim Maddocks

The
COTSWOLD LINE
Worcester to Oxford
Past and Present

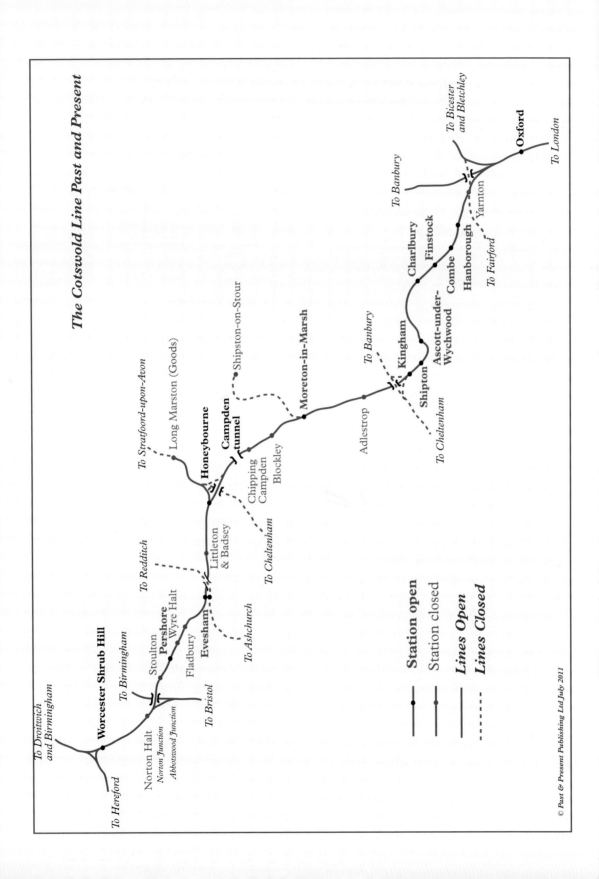

The Cotswold Line Past and Present

Oxford

To London

To Bicester and Bletchley

To Banbury

Yarnton

To Fairford

Charlbury

Finstock

Hanborough

Combe

Ascott-under-Wychwood

Kingham

Shipton

To Banbury

To Cheltenham

Moreton-in-Marsh

Adlestrop

Shipston-on-Stour

Long Marston (Goods)

Campden tunnel

Chipping Campden

Blockley

Honeybourne

To Stratford-upon-Avon

Littleton & Badsey

To Reddich

To Cheltenham

Stoulton

Pershore

Wyre Halt

Fladbury

Evesham

To Ashchurch

Worcester Shrub Hill

To Birmingham

Norton Halt

Norton Junction

Abbotswood Junction

To Bristol

To Drottwich and Birmingham

To Hereford

Station open

Station closed

Lines Open

Lines Closed

© *Past & Present Publishing Ltd July 2011*

A PAST and PRESENT Companion

The
COTSWOLD LINE
Worcester to Oxford
Past and Present

John Stretton
and Tim Maddocks

Past & Present Publishing Ltd

First published in 2011

British Library Cataloguing in Publication Data

A catalogue record for this book is available from the British Library.

ISBN 978 1 85895 275 8

Silver Link Publishing Ltd
The Trundle
Ringstead Road
Great Addington
Kettering
Northants NN14 4BW

Tel/Fax: 01536 330588

email: sales@nostalgiacollection.com

Website: www.nostalgiacollection.com

Printed and bound in the Czech Republic

Acknowledgements

Your authors have always derived great pleasure from 'Past & Present' books, but this one is special, for not only does it have the variety of examining a route (as opposed to, say, a county or preserved line) but it has also enjoyed the backing, cooperation, support and input from so many people within the rail industry, not least Network Rail. In addition to the contribution by Tim Maddocks (whose idea it was to undertake the project), David Northey of Network Rail could not have been more helpful. In addition, the following are also due huge gratitude for their varied and individual help and support: photographers Steve Widdowson, John Whitehouse, Mike Mensing and Neil Beckley; Lee Moyle, for his continual assistance, cooperation and patience; and Owen Karau and other signalmen at Ascott-under-Wychwood and Moreton-in-Marsh.

The book has a slightly different approach from the standard 'Past & Present' volumes, due to the nature of the redoubling project that forms the major feature of the content, but we hope that the reader will appreciate some of the 'behind the scenes' views. Sadly, due to external pressures beyond our control, the cut-off date for the book was before the final pieces of doubling had been completed in some places. We have tried to be as up-to-date as was possible and the book is still a snapshot in time, as are photographs, a car MOT, the Domesday Book and other volumes in the 'Past & Present' series! Peter, David and Will at Silver Link have all played their part in the production, with patience, never-failing courtesy and always with encouragement. Like a football team (and, indeed, a railway system), one needs everyone to be pulling together to create success. We hope the reader feels we have succeeded. Any errors or omissions are ours alone and any comments can be passed to the publisher to correct inaccuracies. Further views of the southern end of the route and into Oxford can be found in John Stretton's *British Railways Past and Present No 55: Oxfordshire – A Second Selection*.

Contents

WORCESTER SHED (85A), at the northern end of our route, provided motive power for much of the local area, as well as top-link passenger locomotives. On 12 July 1964 the shed foreman stands alongside No 4613 as he discusses some matter. Two further '8750' panniers are visible, together with a 'Castle' Class loco on the other side of the shed. Steam was by this time beginning to look very run-down, as evidenced by the somewhat woebegone appearance of No 4613, together with the tatty fireman's long-handled shovel hung on the rear of the bunker! *MJS*

Yes. I remember Adlestrop –
The name, because one afternoon
Of heat the express-train drew up there
Unwontedly. It was late June.

The steam hissed. Someone cleared his throat.
No one left and no one came
On the bare platform. What I saw
Was Adlestrop – only the name…

Like the poet Edward Thomas I too remember Adlestrop. The train I was on was the 3.12pm from Worcester Shrub Hill, and it stopped at all the intermediate stations to Oxford (Adlestrop was between Moreton-in-Marsh and Kingham, and the station house is still there and occupied). It left Oxford at 5.35 and ran non-stop to Paddington, taking exactly an hour. To undergraduates heading to town for a night out it was known as 'The Flying Fornicator'.

My journey was in the early 1960s, and the train was made up of four 1930s Great Western passenger coaches as far as Oxford, with a further two added there, hauled by 'Castle' Class No 7037 *Swindon*. Despite the apparent timelessness of my particular journey – little had changed since the 1920s – it was all about to change. Most of the intermediate stations, like Adlestrop, closed in 1966, following the Beeching Report.

Then there was 'Beeching Mark II', and there was serious discussion about just how small a railway the country could manage with. There were rumours of the Cotswold Line being reduced to two branches at

WORCESTER: One of the enduring features of Worcester Shrub Hill station is the collection of semaphore signals, especially at the western end. One of the gantries stands proudly behind No 50023 *Howe*, in the then new Network SouthEast (NSE) livery, as it departs on Friday 13 June 1986, the NSE launch day, with the 1807 Paddington-Hereford 'Cathedrals Express'. New in May 1968, the loco's name was bestowed at Laira depot after transfer from the Midland to the Western Region ten years later on 17 May 1978. Withdrawn in October 1990, it was stored at Exeter before removal for scrapping. *Steve Widdowson*

each end of the line, and maps were even published on which it had vanished entirely. Passengers, residents, councillors and MPs decided that enough was enough, and resolved in 1972 to do something about it, forming the Cotswold Line Promotion Group. They were not able to prevent the short-sighted singling of the track over much of the route, but at least there was still a service.

User groups tended then to be regarded as troublemakers by railway managers, but they quickly realised that there was something different about the CLPG. Here was a group that genuinely had the railway's interest at heart. They wanted to improve services, not criticise them. They toiled to get more people to take the train, encouraging feeder bus services from nearby villages, they published books on rambles, took stalls at local shows, collected money to improve the appearance of stations, tending flowerbeds and providing plants, and, perhaps most remarkably, successfully made the case for some station reopenings. The biggest prize came in 2008, when Network Rail and the Government agreed to reinstate much of the double track between Charlbury and Evesham. This will lead to substantial improvements in punctuality and reliability, as delays caused by late running in the opposite direction on the single line should be eliminated.

The CLPG membership contains a number of people with serious railway management experience, and they have a particular skill in challenging

assumptions about timetables. Largely thanks to them we should before long have an hourly service all day between Oxford and Worcester, and as a Worcester resident I hope that it will also be possible to slot in a fast service or two in each direction.

In the 1980s, when I was working for the British Railways Board, Jimmy Savile proclaimed – perhaps a little prematurely – 'This is the age of the train'. Maybe then that was an aspiration, rather than a reality. Now it's coming true, as passenger numbers exceed pre-Second World War figures. Electrification, High Speed 2, reinstatement of double track – all these demonstrate that these are good times for the railway. Let's make sure we don't miss out on the Cotswold Line!

WORCESTER SHRUB HILL: Although three years of the 1955 Modernisation Plan had elapsed, bringing the increasing presence of diesel locomotives and multiple units, steam was still very much in charge over the Cotswold Line. 'Hall' No 6992 *Arborfield Hall* takes up the slack and inches its way forward as it restarts a Paddington-Hereford train from Shrub Hill on Sunday 9 March 1958. One of the later-built 'Halls', new in November 1948 and thus a BR loco, it here wears an appropriate 85C (Hereford) shedplate. Withdrawal was in July 1964. *Mike Mensing*

The Cotswold line is seeing a renaissance now, which was unthinkable at the time that I started my railway career. From the general gloom and decline of the 1960s, with line singling and closures, which continued through the 1970s and '80s, there is now an optimistic outlook as the completion of the latest Network Rail-funded double-tracking works moves nearer to final completion – meaning more trains, improved stations and scope for further growth. The completion of the Network Rail Cotswold Line redoubling project comes as UK rail passenger numbers hit the same levels as in the 1920s.

The Cotswold Line renaissance started in a small way in May 1981, with the reopening of Honeybourne station coming five years after the final closure of the Cheltenham to Stratford-upon-Avon link to freight, which had a junction at Honeybourne with the Cotswold Line. Even with that station reopening, however, it wasn't plain sailing due to British Rail's stated intention to withdraw all direct Inter-City trains to and from London over the route from May 1982, due to the alleged poor state of the track; and even during the 1990s, when rail passenger growth was occurring around the country, there was uncertainty facing the line, with closure proposals for Combe and Finstock stations – proposals that were finally withdrawn in May 1994.

Now in 2011 a double-tracked line for most of the route from Oxford to Worcester removes what became a commonplace occurrence in the past, with trains waiting for entry to the single line and a late-running train approaching in the opposite direction, spreading the misery of train delays around the network. The delivered scheme will allow First Great Western to run an enhanced passenger train service from September 2011, serving stations that have also been improved. This happens as the project to refresh the FGW 'Turbo' trains gets into its stride – meaning that, once completed, passengers will have the benefit of smart trains, reliable infrastructure and pleasant stations.

The completed project will also provide an improved level of rail access to the former Ministry of Defence depot at Long Marston, which since 2005 has re-established itself as a location served by most of the UK rail freight operators, hauling rolling stock to and from this location for safe storage or repairs. And the completion of the project opens up a third element, in that special train operators, who have watched the works occur on the route, will be able to bid to run special trains more regularly over the OWW line, using the extra capacity that the double-tracking works have created.

It will be interesting to see what the coming years bring for the OWW route, with rail usage continuing to rise – and a reliable piece of enhanced railway poised to play its part in that continued growth – as we approach the introduction of new trains, electrification and resignalling on the Western Route.

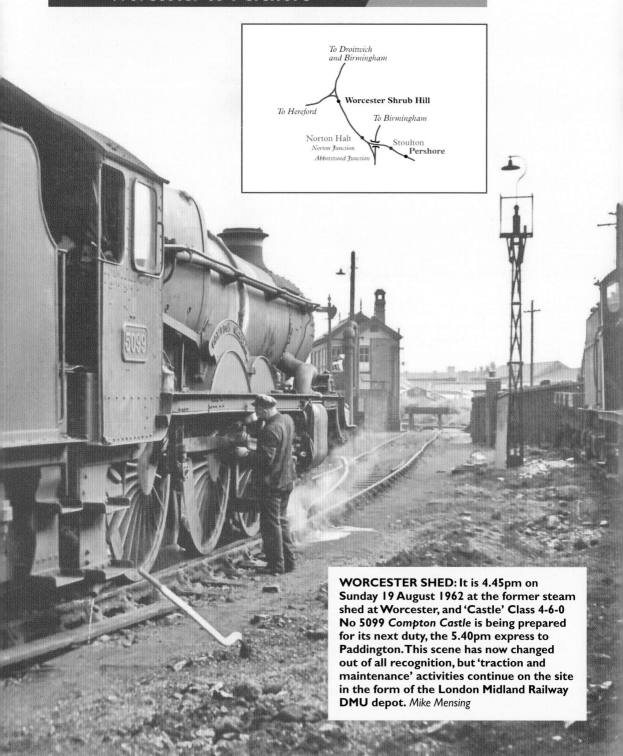

To Droitwich
and Birmingham

Worcester Shrub Hill

To Hereford

To Birmingham

Norton Halt
Norton Junction
Abbotswood Junction

Stoulton
Pershore

WORCESTER SHED: It is 4.45pm on Sunday 19 August 1962 at the former steam shed at Worcester, and 'Castle' Class 4-6-0 No 5099 *Compton Castle* is being prepared for its next duty, the 5.40pm express to Paddington. This scene has now changed out of all recognition, but 'traction and maintenance' activities continue on the site in the form of the London Midland Railway DMU depot. *Mike Mensing*

WORCESTER SHRUB HILL: Looking back in the opposite direction to the view on on page 7, No 4913 *Baglan Hall* rolls to a stand at Shrub Hill on Good Friday, 20 April 1962, with the 5.35pm Hereford-Paddington service. We can see the complex of pointwork that connected the two through platform lines with the middle roads. Modellers will even notice a pair of 'scissors' crossovers in the middle distance, which facilitated the splitting of each through platform for operational purposes.

Moving ahead in time to 22 May 1994, the same angle presents a very different scene. Wearing a respectably clean Railfreight Coal Sector livery, No 58021 stands at the head of duty 1Z54, a Worcester Shrub Hill to Moreton-in-Marsh special. This was the first time a Class 58 loco would work over what was originally the Oxford, Worcester & Wolverhampton (OWW) line, and the run was staged as part of the Worcester Rail Festival. Note the replica 'Cathedrals Express' headboard! *Mike Mensing/Steve Widdowson*

WORCESTER SHRUB HILL: Looking south from the footbridge seen in previous pictures, No 4085 *Berkeley Castle* is a highly unusual sight on second-turn duties, having brought the 12.20pm Oxford-Worcester train into Platform 1 at Shrub Hill on Sunday 9 March 1958. It bears an 81D (Reading) shedplate, denoting its home of many years, but it was officially transferred to Worcester a month later; perhaps the move has already been made. The fireman attends to the tender before its next move.

The station footbridge provides the same viewpoint for this later view, in which an unusual combination of locos, Nos 37254 and 31163, enters the station with 7P57, an engineer's train from Bescot, on 25 January 1998. The intervening years have seen much rationalisation – the two middle roads have been replaced by a single 'middle siding', and all bar one of the carriage sidings beyond Shrub Hill Station signal box have been removed. The former Midland goods shed has been converted to light industrial use. Note what appear to be 'Dogfish' ballast hoppers and a 'Shark' plough van immediately behind the Class 31. The train will run round, then proceed to an engineering worksite at Abbotswood Junction, returning eventually to Bescot. *Mike Mensing/Steve Widdowson*

WORCESTER SHRUB HILL: Another facet of steam days was the sometimes seemingly incessant shunting of empty coaching stock. At 2.30pm on Saturday 29 July 1961 No 4613 shunts a mixed rake of empty stock, while the rest of the station exudes an air of peace and tranquillity. The ex-**GWR** 0-6-0 pannier tank was a long-term servant of Worcester shed, giving value for money until withdrawn on 23 January 1965.

In a rationalised but nonetheless pleasing scene, London Midland Class 150/1 unit No 150125 sits at the London end of the middle siding on 10 November 2010, waiting to form a local service to Birmingham. It is a glorious autumnal day and some **PW** workers are taking advantage of the sunshine in the background to catch up on some maintenance work on the through goods lines. *Mike Mensing/MJS*

WORCESTER SHRUB HILL: In this 2 July 1998 scene No 60046 waits to exit Hereford Siding No 1 at the back of Shrub Hill station. Given that the London-end exit from this set of sidings was controlled by a ground frame, it is likely that this steel train has come up from South Wales via Awre and Abbotswood Junction and has been recessed in the Hereford Sidings to await driver relief before progressing on to Round Oak steel terminal.

Even the goods yard at the back of Shrub Hill station takes on a cheerful appearance in the bright autumn sunshine on 10 November 2010, as PW workers belonging to the local Network Rail Maintenance Delivery Unit continue their work on fettling the trackwork in Hereford Sidings, with No 1 road closest to the centre of the picture and Nos 2 and 3 roads over to the left. All three sidings were part of the DB Schenker (formerly EWS) lease area until recently, but Nos 1 and 3 sidings have now been returned to Network Rail for use by other operators. The actual purpose of the improvement work was to bring the sidings up to standard for the stabling of empty First Great Western (FGW) HST units over the Christmas 2010 holiday period, in connection with amended train working resulting from a major engineering blockade at Reading. The work also included the installation of electrical 'shore supplies' to preheat trains overnight. Although the Hereford Sidings were only initially used by FGW for overnight stabling in December 2010, they were to see further regular overnight usage from May 2011 onwards. *Steve Widdowson/MJS*

WORCESTER SHRUB HILL: Nos 37294 and 37248 double-head an oil train using the avoiding lines through the yard adjoining Shrub Hill station on 20 February 1990, heading north towards the Birmingham area. The Hereford Sidings are immediately to the right of the train, and were still in regular freight use at this time.

A clearer view of the new electric train heating (ETH) installations for **FGW** in the Hereford Sidings behind Shrub Hill station is possible here, as the maintenance gang continues with their work on 10 November 2010. Oil trains are seldom seen at Worcester now, the yard being more normally used for the shunting and stabling of steel and infrastructure trains. There are further sidings (still part of the **DB Schenker** yard lease area) behind the gang, and also the up and down through goods lines between Wyldes Lane and Worcester Tunnel Junction, although some of the yard sidings at this location have been 'mothballed' by **DB Schenker.** *Steve Widdowson/MJS*

WORCESTER: On 9 January 1990 'large logo' No 37012 draws a rake of covered air-braked wagons out of Metal Box Sidings to the east of Shrub Hill station on the up side of the main line.

Autumnal colours abound around the Metal Box siding on 10 November 2010. It is heartening to know that this location is still served by regular freight trains operated by DB Schenker, the rails into the works still retaining a healthy silver sheen. In between the up siding and the up main line can be seen a recently constructed drivers' walking route; this was installed in 2010 to enable drivers of FGW HSTs to change ends in safety, prior to shunting empty HST sets into the 'Back Road' siding behind the station. *Steve Widdowson/MJS*

WORCESTER: '41XX' Class 'Large Prairie' 2-6-2 tank loco No 4113 passes Metal Box Sidings with the 4.45pm departure to Stratford-upon-Avon on Sunday 27 August 1961. The train will run along the OWW main line as far as Honeybourne, before taking the chord to Honeybourne East Loop Junction, Long Marston and Stratford. A long-term resident of Taunton shed, the 'Prairie' was moved to Worcester in November 1953, after just one month at Westbury on the way. The end was officially on 15 January 1966, concomitant with the end of steam on the Western Region at the close of 1965. *Mike Mensing*

NORTON HALT: A Gloucester Railway Carriage & Wagon three-car 'Cross-Country' DMU set (later Class 119) calls at Norton Halt on Saturday 24 August 1963, forming the 2.00pm Stratford to Hereford service. Despite the attraction of travelling in a clean, modern train, the halt has offered up just one customer! Modellers might care to note the somewhat 'piebald' appearance of the platform surfaces – a mixture reflecting a 'patch and mend' approach in the final years of the halt's life, which would eventually end in 1966. The up refuge siding can be seen behind the DMU, stretching back in the Worcester direction.

All trace of the station and the up refuge siding has long since vanished, as 'Turbo' No 165112 accelerates towards Evesham and Oxford. The former single line of the OWW route between Norton Junction and Evesham was controlled in accordance with electric token regulations until the commissioning of the new layout at Evesham West and resignalling in August 2011. Most passenger trains did not, however, have to stop at the signal box to collect or give up the token, due to the existence of a 'repeater' instrument on Shrub Hill station, which allowed the Norton Junction signaller to release a token prior to the booked departure of the train. This was then delivered to the FGW driver by the London Midland platform supervisor, thus

enabling up FGW services bound for Evesham to accelerate to line speed immediately on departing from Worcester. This practice saved valuable minutes in the schedule of each train. Following the 2011 new works, however, the single line became signalled in accordance with track circuit block regulations, which do not require trains to carry a token, the clearance of the signal being the driver's authority to proceed onto the single line. *Mike Mensing/MJS*

NORTON JUNCTION: A three-car DMU from the **OWW** route accelerates away from Norton Junction in 1963. The driver's window is still open after handing the electric token to the signalman, although perhaps he will now keep it open all the way to Worcester, in order to enjoy the warm weather.

The extent of the rationalisation of the junction layout at Norton is apparent in this view dated 5 April 1987, as a Class 117 DMU forms a down service for Worcester passing the signal box. The train will run over the up line for a short distance behind the photographer, before regaining the down line through a crossover. Note that the signal box still retains its traditional wooden-framed windows in this view! Modellers should note the point rodding and the wooden board crossing, provided to allow the signalman to manually exchange tokens with freight and other non-passenger trains that were not booked to pick up or deliver their single-line token at Shrub Hill station. *Mike Mensing/Steve Widdowson*

NORTON JUNCTION: We now move ahead again, to 8 August 1995, as 'Thames Turbo' unit No 166202, forming a down service, slows for the permanent speed restriction through the crossover behind the photographer. A feature of the modern scene is the orange 'Under Track Crossing' pipe immediately in front of the signal box, which protects an important cable route from accidental damage during any track works in the vicinity.

'Turbo' unit No 165112 diverges from the Abbotswood Junction line at Norton Junction and runs towards Pershore and Evesham with an up working on 9 April 2011. Note that the signal box has by now acquired new double-glazed window units. These are said to be much more efficient at keeping out the winter draughts, but sadly in our view do nothing for the aesthetic appearance of the building. *Steve Widdowson/ MJS*

NORTON JUNCTION: Privatisation is just under a year away as 'Dutch'-liveried No 31516 leads a stablemate on a down ballast working past the signal box on 20 April 1993, although judging by the empty appearance of the wagons this train has probably completed its work, or is simply being worked empty to another yard to be reloaded for the following weekend's engineering work. The effects of emerging Health & Safety regulations are evident in this view: the board crossing has had a non-slip surface applied and its edges lined in white.

No 47478 appears to be on an identical working on 10 February 1995. Modellers of the more modern scene will note the temporary orange 'netlon' fence adjacent to the down line, no doubt installed to provide a safe walking route to a work site. Another seldom-modelled feature is the driver's 'hi-vis' jacket folded up in the windscreen of the locomotive! *Both Steve Widdowson*

NORTON JUNCTION: The pre-rationalisation junction layout is shown to good effect in this 1966 view, in which a three-car DMU, forming an up service, takes the Cotswold Line. The unit is still in a rather shabby green livery, albeit with small yellow ends; a full repaint into the new BR 'Corporate Blue' can surely not be far off. The double track to Abbotswood Junction on the Bristol to Birmingham main line leads off in the foreground.

The old corporate colours of British Rail began to give way to the new InterCity 'Executive' livery, which adorns No 47612 *Titan* and some of its coaches in this view at Norton Junction on 17 May 1987, as they form the 1615 (SuO) Hereford to Paddington express. *Mike Mensing/Steve Widdowson*

STOULTON was the first station on the **OWW** main line after leaving **Norton Junction**. Opened in 1854, it was located in a rural setting more than a mile from the village it served. In 1905 one Edward Upstone is recorded as being the station master here. On Saturday 24 August 1963 a Derby three-car WR 'Suburban' DMU set (later Class 116) approaches Stoulton station as the 5.50pm service from Worcester Shrub Hill to Stratford-upon-Avon.

More than 30 years later, on 17 July 1994, the view is much the same, with the significant exception that the railway here was singled in 1971. The train and motive power are, however, rather different! Res Parcels Sector-liveried No 47765 is coupled ahead of No 5029 *Nunney Castle*, working 1Z40, a Flying Scotsman Services charter train from Southampton to Worcester. The diesel was summoned up from Bristol and attached to the return train at Worcester due to the unfortunate fact that No 5029 had caused so many lineside fires on the outward journey between Didcot and Worcester. *Mike Mensing/Steve Widdowson*

STOULTON: 'Hymek' No D7060 passes Stoulton station on Saturday 24 August 1963 with the 3.15pm Paddington to Hereford service. New from Beyer Peacock in December 1962, and allocated to Cardiff Canton shed, its operational life was to be less than ten years, a victim of BR's decision to rid itself of diesel-hydraulic locomotives.

Together with several other OWW stations, Stoulton closed in January 1966. Nearly 48 years later no trace of the station remains, although the surrounding rural landscape remains as pleasant as ever. No 166203, very smart in one of the later FGW liveries and forming the 1321 Paddington-Great Malvern service, passes the site on 9 April 2011. *Mike Mensing/MJS*

STOULTON: On 30 November 1984
a broken fishplate near milepost 115
at Stoulton caused the derailment
of 1A20, the 0705 Hereford to
Paddington train, worked by
Class 47 No 47500 *Great Western*.
Although the locomotive wasn't
derailed, a number of carriages
did come off the road and there
was considerable track damage,
resulting in the line being closed for
three days.

In the second view, taken on the
same day, No 47500 and the non-
derailed coaches have already been
worked away from the site, and
railway officials in orange jackets
assess the situation. Fortunately
there were no fatalities in this
accident, although six passengers
sustained injuries. Later that day
classmate No 47100 brought a
breakdown train up from Old Oak
Common to recover the damaged
vehicles. *Both Steve Widdowson*

PERSHORE: Seen from the road overbridge at the Worcester end of the station, No 166212 of Thames Trains, with silver roof, approaches Pershore on 21 February 1999 forming the 1512 (SuO) Great Malvern to Paddington service.

Some 12 years later the scene is almost unchanged, apart from the greater lineside growth, as stablemate No 166214 approaches Pershore station as the 0943 Great Malvern to Paddington service. The industrial building on the left remains and the down 'cess' has acquired an 'HST Stop' board, which indicates to drivers where to stop the cab of the leading power car on down trains. *Steve Widdowson/MJS*

PERSHORE: Class 50 'Hoover' No 50045 passes Pershore station on Jubilee Bank Holiday, 7 June 1977, with the 1250 Paddington to Worcester Shrub Hill train, consisting of nine Mark 2 air-conditioned coaches. The loco was named *Achilles* the following April, but lost that identity very briefly in 1989. Its end came on 11 December 1990. Little remains of the former up platform; the station buildings were demolished in 1970 and all trains have used the down platform only since the line was singled in 1971. The area behind the up platform used to be a goods yard of two sidings. A goods loop also ran around the back of the platform, but this was all removed following the cessation of goods services in the 1960s.

Three coaches suffice on 9 April 2011, as No 166214 arrives at Pershore as the 0943 Great Malvern-Paddington service. The signal troughing route is still extant in the up 'cess', and the platform has acquired a yellow 'safety line'. The biggest contrast, however, lies outside the current railway boundary fence, where a large industrial building has been constructed on the former goods yard in recent years. Happily, the trademark **GWR** pine trees remain! *Mike Mensing/MJS*

PERSHORE: No 47294 heads non-stop through Pershore on Sunday 26 August 1979 with the 1625 Hereford to Paddington express. Note what appear to be the original station platform lights. Pershore was planned for closure at the same time as Honeybourne in 1969, but was fortunately reprieved following the publication of a report indicating that severe hardship would be caused for Worcester passengers.

On 15 November 2008 power car No 43143 brings up the rear of 1W17, the 0851 Paddington-Great Malvern service, as it departs from Pershore. Despite the happy survival of the fir trees on the site of the former up platform, the scene is now dominated by the new industrial buildings on the right. Although the platform lighting has been renewed since the 1979 view, it is interesting to note that the lighting units appear to be mounted on the same posts as before. *Mike Mensing/MJS*

PERSHORE: Unit No 150270 calls at Pershore on 30 March 1989, forming the 1416 Hereford to Oxford service. Prior to the introduction of the Class 165/166 'Turbo' units on the line, 'Sprinter'-type units worked local services. At this time in the station's history, there was a long 3-hour gap in services in the middle of the day, which Pershore Town Council had been pressing British Rail to fill and also to provide more trains at other times of the day. *Steve Widdowson*

PERSHORE: On 3 April 1990 ex-LNER 'K4' Class No 3442 *The Great Marquess* **passes Pershore with its support coach, in a transit movement between Didcot and Kidderminster, for a period of use on the Severn Valley Railway.**
   On 22 June 2003 Pershore has a newly installed running-in board. The sign was jointly paid for by Thames Trains and a local company, Flowserve-Valtek, based on the other side of the road bridge, and was unveiled on 5 May 2002 by TV personality Alistair McGowan. That day marked the 150th

anniversary of the line as far as Evesham, with a special 'Thames Turbo' unit (No 166212) running from Stourbridge Junction to Evesham, picking up VIPs and invited guests for the main event at Evesham. *Both Steve Widdowson*

PERSHORE: This general view of the station looking towards Worcester on 24 July 1968 shows how things used to be. Despite still looking complete, the weeds on the up platform reflect the fact that the line has begun to be run down. This rural-looking scene belies the fact that the station is quite close to the town, although actually situated in Pinvin.

In the contrasting view on 9 April 2011 part of the old up platform remains in situ, and a concrete troughing route now occupies part of the former up-line formation. Much of the 1968 vegetation has been removed and a small car park created for station users. An industrial building has sprung up in the background, built on former railway land. *Robin Leleux/MJS*

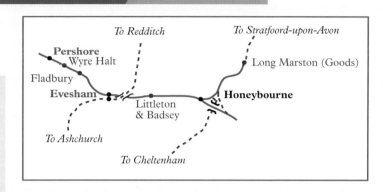

To Redditch   To Stratfoord-upon-Avon

Pershore

Wyre Halt   Long Marston (Goods)

Fladbury

Evesham   **Honeybourne**

Littleton & Badsey

To Ashchurch

To Cheltenham

WYRE HALT:
Respectably clean 'Hymek' D7048 powers through Wyre Halt on 24 August 1963 with the 4.05pm Hereford-Paddington train, consisting of a rake of maroon Mark I coaches. As can be seen, the halt was of the most rudimentary nature, being mainly constructed of timber. It was closed in January 1966, together with a number of other OWW stations. New on 6 October 1962, to Bristol Bath Road depot, D7048 spent time at both Old Oak Common and Newport Ebbw Junction before withdrawal in January 1972. It was cut up at Swindon Works just seven months later. *Mike Mensing*

Amidst delightful rural surroundings No 47500 heads away from the site of Wyre Halt on Sunday 26 August 1979 with the 1625 Paddington-Hereford express. The loco, here carrying slightly larger-style numbers, together with the name *Great Western,* **which had been applied six months earlier, was renumbered 47770 on 27 May 1994, and renamed** *Reserved* **in July of that year.** *Mike Mensing*

WYRE HALT: Through a deceptively narrow corridor, HST power car No 43181 *Devonport Royal Dockyard 1693-1993* heads a Great Western Trains set in the attractive green and ivory livery past the site of Wyre Halt on Sunday 7 February 1999, working the 1045 Paddington-Hereford service. Taken from the road overbridge seen in the previous photograph, the contrast with the 1963 view could not be greater – the halt has been completely swept away and it is as if it had never been.

More than 12 years have passed since the previous view, and the vegetation has not been idle! Passing the site of Wyre Halt, an unidentified **FGW HST** set heads west, forming the 0821 Paddington-Great Malvern service of 9 April 2011. One other change is the new troughing route installed in the down 'cess'. There are currently no plans to redouble this section between Evesham and Norton Junction. *Steve Widdowson/MJS*

FLADBURY: Birmingham Railway Carriage & Wagon Bo-Bo diesel-electric (now Class 33) No D6533 passes Fladbury station at 2.55pm on Saturday 18 May 1963 with an up fitted Esso oil tanker train. Note the very open aspect and the two wooden-bodied open wagons serving as 'barrier' vehicles, formerly a requirement that served to separate locomotive from potentially volatile product.

Was there ever a station here? Now on a route that is ordinarily devoid of through freight, No 166216 heads east past the site of Fladbury station forming the 1432 Great Malvern-Paddington service of 9 April 2011. The station closed in January 1966 and the passage of time has eradicated virtually all traces of it. Double track was to reach almost this location again in August 2011, when the redoubling scheme restored a second track as far as Gishbourne Farm User Worked Crossing, a farm access crossing approximately a mile west of Evesham. *Mike Mensing/MJS*

EVESHAM: Signaller Graham Dargie waits to hand the Evesham to Norton Junction electric token to the driver of a down train outside Evesham signal box on 25 September 2002. Although this token gives the driver authority to occupy the single line between these points, the train will not stop at Norton Junction to hand it in. Rather, to save the time lost by stopping, the token will be restored to the system in an Auxiliary Token Instrument located at Worcester Shrub Hill station. Just beyond where the signaller is standing was the former junction with the Midland line from Ashchurch to Evesham and Redditch.

We visit Evesham box again on 2 October 2010, and can see that the scene has changed little in the intervening time. Modellers of the contemporary scene will note the point rodding and signaller's walkway, complete with safety surface and edge lining. The little-used siding on the right was used for the stabling of tampers and other on-track plant in recent years. Together with the other remaining siding at Evesham, it will be removed as part of the current redoubling project, with new siding facilities being provided at Honeybourne instead. *Phil Marsh/ MJS*

EVESHAM: In a delightful memory from the past, a three-car WR 'Suburban' DMU set arrives at Evesham on Saturday 14 April 1962 as the 2.50pm service from Worcester Shrub Hill. The DMU is still in its original BR all-over green livery. Note the goods yard to the right of the train with what would become a Class 03 diesel shunter, No D2136, employed on shunting duties. The 1961 wooden signal box stands in the background, overlooking the junction with the former Midland lines on the left.

Slightly later in the day, at 4.10pm, No D2136 has emerged from the sidings and is captured drawing vans out of a siding at Evesham GWR. *Both Mike Mensing*

EVESHAM: No 50041 *Bulwark* approaches Evesham off the single-line section from Norton Junction in May 1982, just prior to the withdrawal of most of the locomotive-hauled services from the route. The goods shed has now gone, together with the former goods yard, part of which (to the extreme right) appears to have been sold and fenced off. Of the junction with the ex-Midland lines there is now little trace apart from the expanse of scrubland to the left of the new fence. No 50041 was later involved in an accident on the approach to Paddington on the morning of 23 November 1983 while working the up 'Night Riviera' sleeping car train from Penzance, when it ran through a series of points at speed and was derailed.

Some 29 years later, on 9 April 2011, the basic rail corridor is relatively unchanged, but with development on surrounding land, as FGW's No 43144 heads an up service for London Paddington past the signal box. Note that the site of the former junction with the Ashchurch line has now disappeared under a new access road and that the site of the up sidings is occupied by a set of new PW offices behind the signal box. The down line has also been recently relaid, as part of the preparations for the redoubling works. The new double track from Moreton-in-Marsh will eventually extend approximately 1 mile to the west of Evesham, to Gishbourne Farm User Worked Crossing. The signal box will remain to control the rebuilt railway as far as Honeybourne, but semaphore signals will not survive and will be replaced by colour light signals in slightly different locations. *John Whitehouse/MJS*

EVESHAM: A slightly wider angle on the scene witnesses Fowler 2-6-4T No 42416 approaching Evesham Midland station on Saturday 14 April 1962 with the 4.30pm Ashchurch to Redditch service. The previously seen ex-GWR lines are on the right, behind the nearer rake of goods wagons. *Mike Mensing*

Moments later, and turning through roughly 180 degrees, we see No 42416 arriving at Evesham Midland. Note the fairly extensive facilities for freight at this Midland outpost, and the ex-GWR station to the left. *Mike Mensing*

EVESHAM: Western motive power has crept into the rosters over the ex-Midland route, as low-roofed '57XX' pannier tank No 8743 departs from Evesham Midland with the 3.41pm service to Ashchurch on Saturday 18 May 1963; a single Stanier coach suffices for the traffic on offer. The up and down station buildings of the GWR station, together with the footbridge, are clearly visible in the background. No 8743 was a well-travelled engine, oscillating in BR days between South Wales, the West Midlands and London. Its end came from Old Oak Common on 22 November 1964. *Mike Mensing*

EVESHAM: An elegant Midland Railway footbridge frames the MR-designed platform canopy in this view of Evesham Midland station taken on 13 September 1956, looking towards Ashchurch; the GWR station is out of view to the right. The line to Ashchurch remained open to passenger traffic until 17 June 1963, although goods traffic continued to use the Midland yard at Evesham via the connection with the GWR line until 1967. *Richard Casserley*

Top: **EVESHAM: Fowler 2-6-4 tank loco No 42416 is seen again as it stands in the former Midland station at Evesham on 14 April 1962 with the 4.30pm train from Ashchurch to Redditch, consisting of Stanier steel-bodied coaches. The section from Evesham to Redditch via Broome Junction did not have long to live at this point, closing to rail passenger services on 1 October 1962, due to poor track condition; a substitute bus service ran for a while longer and goods services initially continued to serve Studley and Alcester stations. Note the ex-GWR station in the background, an access road and car park separating the main buildings of the respective stations.**

Main picture: **A direct comparative view is unfortunately no longer possible due to housing development and the growth of vegetation, but this view of the former GWR station taken on 9 April 2011 gives an impression of how this scene has changed over the last 50 years. The original railway boundary fencing seen here in the far left foreground is that shown in the right background of the 1962 photograph.** *Mike Mensing/MJS*

EVESHAM: An unidentified Class 50 in standard British Rail 'Corporate Blue' draws into the ex-GWR station at Evesham on an unspecified date in 1982 with a down express service, composed mainly of air-conditioned Mark 2 coaches. Note the up siding snaking past the rear of the up platform. The Railway Hotel occupies a

dominant position as it looks down on the station. Until 1963 this would have served customers from both stations; the Midland line passed immediately to the right of the hotel, and the parapet of the bridge carrying the road over the line is just visible.

The same view on 9 April 2011 shows the extent to which new building development has changed the skyline of Evesham itself, although the Railway Hotel building remains at the top of the station approach road. FGW 'Turbo' unit No 165112 is about to depart towards Worcester; the door to the token hut on the down platform appears to be open, so no doubt the driver is within, obtaining the signaller's permission to withdraw the electric token to Norton Junction. Both lines through the platforms have already been relaid as part of the Cotswold redoubling scheme, and new lengths of long welded rail have been laid in the 'four-foot' of the down line, prior to being used in the next phase of the scheme in August 2011, when the double track will be extended from Moreton-in-Marsh through to Gishbourne Farm User Worked Crossing, a mile west of Evesham station. *John Whitehouse/MJS*

EVESHAM: Seen from the road bridge immediately west of the station, a Gloucester RCW double-ended car (W55000 series, later Class 122) and a driving trailer leave Evesham GWR forming the 4.00pm Stratford-upon-Avon to Worcester service on Saturday 14 April 1962.

The same view on 19 April 1987 shows 'large logo'-liveried Class 50 No 50010 *Monarch* easing the 16.10 Paddington to Hereford service away from its station stop. The pile of empty barrels and wooden pallets roughly corresponds to the site of the long-demolished goods shed, while off picture to the right is where the town's Midland station stood. The former GWR shunters' cabins in the background still appear to be in use, while a new prefabricated building for PW use has appeared in the background. The trailing connection to the two remaining (up) sidings at Evesham is hidden behind the locomotive. *Mike Mensing/John Whitehouse*

EVESHAM: The shape of things to come: on 3 May 1993 a pristine No 166203 had the distinction of being the first Class 166 'Turbo' to work over the Cotswold Line on a crew-training run between Worcester and Oxford, and is seen here arriving at Evesham. 'Turbos' started working service trains over the OWW route from the introduction of the 1993 Summer timetable on 17 May. The original bullhead track of the up line seems to have been freshly ballasted.

A more elevated view sees No 43069 arriving at Evesham at the head of the 1406 Worcester Shrub Hill to Paddington service on 30 September 2010. Both the up and down loops in Evesham station had recently been relaid in connection with preparations for the redoubling project. The old up siding in the background was not to be so lucky, and was due to be finally removed in August 2011. The old shunters' cabins are still standing, although currently disused, with the PW offices having been moved to new accommodation at the rear of the signal box a couple of years previously. *Steve Widdowson/MJS*

EVESHAM: In a scene redolent of model railway perfection, Evesham **GWR** station basks in the early autumn sunshine on 13 September 1956. Some of the buildings still appear to be in Great Western light and dark stone colours. Rationalisation and the Beeching Report are still some years away and business on the railway here appears to be in good health. An ex-GWR box van sits ahead of a BR standard van in the down-side dock siding and the goods yard in the distance is full of wagons. A down train is just departing for Worcester. Note the original signal box in the foreground, still in operational use.

More than 40 years have elapsed since the previous view, as a relatively new No 66028, wearing the livery of English, Welsh & Scottish Railway (EWS), draws into the station with an up charter train on 27 February 1999. The siding behind the up platform lingers on, but the old signal box and down dock siding have long since disappeared, the former replaced by the 'modern' Western Region wooden example at the Worcester end of the station. *Richard Casserley/Steve Widdowson*

EVESHAM: Over the weekend of 2/3 October 2010 a major engineering possession took place between Evesham and Moreton-in-Marsh, to enable work to be undertaken on two important bridges at Common, just east of Evesham, and at Honeybourne. In this view, looking back towards Evesham station, construction staff employed by Amey Colas at Common overbridge pause to take stock on 2 October. Note the profusion of yellow plant in this scene, which has been engaged in removing the track and ballast from the bridge itself, to enable a new waterproof membrane to be installed above the brick arches.

Turning 180 degrees from the previous view on the same day, the new membrane over the bridge is clearly visible. The bridge crosses a track and care was taken during the planning and execution of the job to ensure that no debris or other materials could fall onto the path below. Although still single-track in this view, the railway here will again be double-track when the project is completed. *Both MJS*

CLAYFIELD CROSSING: Preparations for the redoubling project continue, as work takes place at Clayfield Crossing, east of Littleton & Badsey, during a possession on Sunday 10 October 2010 to excavate a new cable troughing route. The redoubling work has required a considerable amount of resignalling and telecoms works, which has been installed by Amey on behalf of Network Rail.

In the second view, from Tuesday 14 June 2011, the preparation work is completed, with track laid and ballast dropped ready for the final push towards and over the level crossing here during the August blockade. Note how close the trajectory of the line is to the erstwhile crossing keeper's house!

The third view is looking west, also on 14 June 2011, showing the former crossing keeper's house at Clayfield Crossing. From this angle the new track looks destined to invade the house's garden! The crossing conveys a minor road between Bretforton and Littleton over the railway and is now automated. When the railway is redoubled, all public vehicular level crossings will feature coated rails, clips and housings to help avoid corrosion from road salt. *All MJS*

IVY LANE CROSSING: We now move slightly further east on 10 October 2010, but retain our westward-looking aspect as we find more cable troughing work taking place at Ivy Lane User Worked Crossing. Palletised concrete troughing lids have been delivered to the formation of the former up line, to the right of the picture, and are awaiting installation.

Turning through 180 degrees, we see a team of Amey staff and associated heavy plant working further along the line in the Honeybourne direction. The Amey Colas track renewal teams would visit this location some six months later to excavate the former up-line trackbed and prepare it to receive track again. This was then laid by May 2011, in readiness for the major blockade in August, when it would be connected up at either end and commissioned, ready for use. *Both MJS*

HONEYBOURNE: This view to the west of the old platform at Honeybourne on 21 April 2009, looking east towards Moreton-in-Marsh, shows the abandoned island platform left of centre. The tracks from the old sidings, out of view to the left, passing under the left-hand road overbridge, are here not in use. This bridge and the left-hand platform face will eventually be available to the Gloucestershire Warwickshire heritage railway when it extends to this point, and also provide realigned access for trains to Long Marston after the doubling.

On 13 September 2010 FGW power car No 43148 powers up after departing from the Honeybourne station stop with a midday down working. The area to the right of the train in this view used to be railway land, but was sold off for redevelopment following the original run-down and closure of the station in British Rail days. The present housing development rather hems in the present-day station, restricting the size of the car park. The track panels on the left were recovered from relaying sites elsewhere on the OWW route a few months earlier, and are mostly earmarked for the relaying of the three up sidings at Honeybourne, which is part of the present redoubling project. *Tim Maddocks/MJS*

HONEYBOURNE: BR Standard Class 9F 2-10-0 No 92235 of Ebbw Junction shed stands on the up main line at Honeybourne station in the early 1960s. Also visible in the former loco siding is an unidentified 'Hall' 4-6-0. Honeybourne used to have its own loco shed in the vicinity of the coaling stage behind the 'Hall', but this was closed in the early years of the 20th century and was demolished in 1907. No 92235 lasted almost until the end of Western Region steam; withdrawn from Bristol Barrow Road shed in November 1965, it was cut up in April 1966.

9Fs no longer grace the OWW route, but from the same viewpoint as the previous picture we see FGW 'Turbo' unit No 166215 slowing for the station stop with an up service on 13 September 2010. New concrete troughing units are stored on the formation of the former up main line, waiting to be installed a few weeks later; that line will then be relaid through the station, resulting in the old up main platform being rebuilt to modern standards. *MJS collection/MJS*

HONEYBOURNE: Also on 13 September 2010 we see the passenger 'bus shelter', which would be replaced by a more modern version a few weeks later as part of the overall route upgrading carried out by Network Rail and First Great Western. An original GWR platform bench seems to have survived the culls of the post-Beeching era, and the floral display maintained by the local station supporters group adds a splash of welcome colour.

On the bitterly cold morning of 7 February 2011 contract workers are busy installing the new platform shelter, which comes as a kit of parts from the manufacturer. The old 1970s-pattern 'bus shelter' has already been removed and the site prepared. Note the proximity of the new housing behind the station.

The photographer returned a few hours later to check on progress and found the new shelter more or less erected and seemingly just awaiting the installation of the side glazing panels. *MJS/Tim Maddocks (2)*

HONEYBOURNE: The old goods yard on the up side to the rear of Honeybourne station remains firmly in the grip of rampant vegetation on 13 September 2010, having last been used (by the Civil Engineer) approximately 10 years earlier. Underneath the jungle there are three sidings, still physically connected to the network! This level of disuse would normally spell the end for sidings such as these, but Honeybourne was identified as the optimum location for tamper and on-track machine (OTM) stabling and servicing on the OWW route. As a result, the two sidings at Evesham, and two of the three at Moreton-in-Marsh, were to be removed and the connections plain-lined as part of the redoubling project during the summer of 2011. These sidings at Honeybourne will be relaid with 'second-hand' serviceable track from elsewhere in the area at the same time, and brought back into use.

On the same day a party of Network Rail and Amey Colas engineers discusses the forthcoming work necessary to bring the three sidings at Honeybourne back into use, as a FGW HST passes in the background with a down service. The term 'personal protective equipment' (PPE) was certainly justified in view of the profusion of brambles and other 'hazardous greenery'!

By the time the third view was taken on 9 April 2011 the sidings area had been totally transformed. Amey Colas PW gangs have removed all the vegetation apparent in the earlier photographs and have moved the track panels previously stored next to the running line into position for eventual relaying. As already mentioned, three long sidings will be provided for the stabling and servicing of tampers and other OTMs, and also for possible freight usage in the future.
All MJS

HONEYBOURNE: On 21 November 1970 a three-car DMU set (Nos 50304, 59115, 50338) is seen in the former 'Down Stratford' line platform at Honeybourne, with the RCTS 'The Cotswold Edge Railtour'. This had departed from Birmingham New Street at 0935 to Gloucester Docks and various other goods-only lines in the Gloucester area via Bromsgrove, Droitwich Spa and Ashchurch. The train returned via the Cheltenham to Stratford line, but also ran up from Honeybourne West Loop Junction to Honeybourne station and back, before proceeding on to Birmingham via Long Marston and Stratford-upon-Avon. Honeybourne station itself was well and truly disused by this time, having finally closed to passenger traffic on 5 May 1969, although there still appears to be goods traffic in the yard beyond the station. The former Stratford platforms had by now been truncated at the Worcester end and, apart from

access to the goods sidings, were retained as a run-round loop for trains accessing West Loop Junction and vice versa. Note the old coal yard to the left of the picture, occupying an area that would eventually be built on with housing.

On 24 April 1982 No 50037 *Illustrious* approaches Honeybourne with the 1603 Worcester-Paddington service. All else is desolation, with wide open spaces all around! The former down main platform is again in good condition, having been reopened to passenger services on 22 May 1981, but the island platform slumbers on in quiet dereliction, waiting for its rebirth 30 years later. The old coal yard has disappeared and the goods sidings in the background seem devoid of traffic, although the connection was still operational at this time. The junction signal in the foreground is cleared for the up direction towards Moreton-in-Marsh. The arm at 'danger' controls the connection to the Long Marston line at Honeybourne West Loop Junction, but appearances are deceptive, as the former signal box effectively only retained the status of a ground frame and was normally only manned at this time when a movement was booked to or from Long Marston. *Hugh Ballantyne/John Whitehouse*

HONEYBOURNE: The scene at Honeybourne looking towards Worcester on 10 October 2010 illustrates well the way that nature has taken over parts of the old station area in the intervening 28 years. Still visible is the concrete troughing route along the line of the former up main line, which appeared to have been only recently installed in the 1982 view. Housing has sprung up in the left background and a small car park provided adjacent to the operational platform. When the station reopened in 1981 the original length of the former down platform was not restored, it being more cost-effective to restore a shorter one. Although modern rail industry standards mean that the up main face of the old island platform must be reopened to the full length of an eight-car HST, the existence of 'Grandfather Rights', together with the relatively recent provision of selective door opening on HST coaches, means that there are no current plans to extend the existing single platform. The former Stratford platforms moulder on, the track in this view having been taken out of use in the early

2000s. As part of the redoubling project, the junction with the Long Marston line will be remodelled and moved from its current location east of the station to the Worcester end. The through line to Long Marston will be relaid with 'new' second-hand serviceable track and will run along the alignment of the right-hand of the two disused lines in this photo. The left-hand track will be lifted and the alignment safeguarded for future use by the Gloucestershire Warwickshire heritage railway.

Eight months later the trackbed on the extreme right is being prepared for the relaying of track for Long Marston; new lengths of track rest in the 'four-foot' of the down line; the new waiting shelter is on the down platform; track panels with concrete sleepers and stacks of metal sleepers await their turn for attention in the middle distance; and the ballast of the second track can been seen in the distance. Elsewhere the island platform still slumbers as No 166221 arrives as the 0954 Great Malvern-Paddington service on 14 June 2011. *Both MJS*

HONEYBOURNE: Wearing Railfreight 'Sectorisation' livery, No 31271 is on a crew training run on 17 December 1992 from Bescot to Honeybourne Tip, which was about to be reopened for use by the Civil Engineer. On the single OWW main line No 43122 passes with a Paddington to Great Malvern express. The Long Marston line diverges to the left out of shot in the distance behind the HST. In the foreground, between the two lines, is the ground frame that controlled access to the branch from the OWW main line. The hut contained a remote token instrument and a telephone to Evesham signal box. A freight service wishing to access the Long Marston line would normally be routed via Worcester and would stop on the approach to the ground frame, where the shunter would request a release of the frame from the signalman. When the movement was clear of the OWW main line, the shunter would return the points to the 'normal' position (i.e. set for the main line) and would restore the electric token to the machine in the hut. The train for Long Marston or Honeybourne Tip would thus be 'locked in' on the branch and could then proceed on its way or shunt the sidings in the Honeybourne area, without interfering with the passage of passenger trains on the main line.

The same view on Saturday 9 April 2011 again shows an HST on a down service, this time No 43181 slowing for the stop at Honeybourne with the 1021 Paddington to Hereford service. The ground frame is still operational, with the line to Long Marston disappearing off into the distance as before. The old single track that led back to the former Stratford line platforms at the station, however, has been removed in preparation

for the remodelling of the whole junction and layout. This will see a new fully signalled junction and main-to-main crossover installed to the west of the station, worked from the new mini-panel in Evesham signal box. The Long Marston line will run through the former northernmost platform alignment at Honeybourne station and will be slewed over as required to create a future 'path' for the Gloucestershire Warwickshire heritage railway, which will come up from the former West Loop Junction, under the OWW main line and around a rebuilt alignment adjacent to the now-closed tip. The existing ground frame and associated infrastructure will be removed at the same time. The new works will also include a restored connection to the former goods sidings to the north-west of the station, reopened during August 2011 as a tamper stabling and light maintenance facility for the OWW line, as well as providing for the future stabling and shunting of freight traffic on and off the Long Marston line. *Steve Widdowson/MJS*

HONEYBOURNE BRIDGE:
Approximately half a mile east of Honeybourne the OWW line passed over the Cheltenham to Stratford main line. Following closure of the latter in 1976, the chord line from Honeybourne station to West Loop Junction was initially retained to provide a connection for freight traffic to and from Long Marston MoD Depot, which remained rail-connected. West Loop signal box was also kept in use for several years, being manned 'as required'

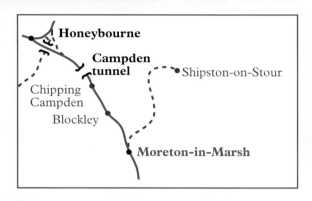

Looking from the same point on 9 April 2011, the new bridge is in place and in use. The temporary road surface, Portakabins and all other evidence of the construction site have been completely removed and a no doubt relieved farmer goes about his business. *Both MJS*

for Long Marston traffic. The retention of the Long Marston connection under the OWW meant that, when the latter was singled in 1971, the life-expired former double-track bridge had to be replaced, rather than simply filling the gap in with earthworks. The replacement steel girder bridge only needed to be for a single track, however, and this in turn was replaced over the weekend of 2/3 October 2010 as part of the on-going preparations for redoubling the line. The civil engineering works for this and Common bridge at Evesham were carried out by Birse Rail on behalf of Network Rail. This was the entrance to the site on 10 October. The new double-track span can be seen in readiness to the left of the original.

HONEYBOURNE BRIDGE: Another view of the Birse Rail compound taken on 13 September 2010, shortly prior to the installation of the new bridge, shows the extent of temporary roadway necessary to effect the successful completion of these works. One important reason for using temporary road panels such as this was to allow the huge items of civil engineering plant required for the lift easy access to the site.

The second view shows the farmer continuing to plough his reclaimed land on 9 April 2011.

In the third picture preparations for the big bridge lift on 2 October 2010 are well in hand in the Birse Rail compound as the 1206 Worcester Foregate Street to Paddington service crosses the old single-track span on 30 September 2010. *All MJS*

HONEYBOURNE BRIDGE:
On Thursday 30 September 2010 the new double-track span has been raised up on temporary supports, waiting to be installed during the engineering blockade that would start the following night. It needed to be at the height illustrated so that the massive tracked jacking equipment could move itself underneath the span, prior to lifting it up and moving it across the site to the railway. The new bridge was assembled on site from a number of prefabricated,

reinforced concrete girder sections, which had been manufactured in Ireland and shipped to the site at Honeybourne. The old single-track span sees out its final day of service in the background.

We move slightly closer to the line on the morning of Saturday 2 October 2010, only to find that the old bridge has disappeared overnight! It is 0918, and preparations are proceeding exactly to plan for the installation of the new span. More temporary roadway plates have been laid on the mud of the farmer's field to allow the enormous tracked machines to carry the new double-track span into position. Note the new concrete abutments, which were constructed with steel reinforcements in front of the originals. The GWR abutments, built of engineers blue brick, are now buried inside the new concrete structures that were required to carry the weight of the new span. *Both MJS*

HONEYBOURNE BRIDGE: We rewind by 1 minute to 0917 on Saturday 2 October 2010 and turn the camera by almost 180 degrees to see a piece of civil engineering plant of truly gargantuan proportions carrying the new reinforced concrete double-track span. The original single-track steel span has already been removed and placed on temporary plinths, pending its removal from the site to a new home on the Telford Steam Railway.

The methodology becomes clear a short while later, as the tracked lifting gear has moved the new span almost into position, and is about to lower it into its final resting place – far more skilful than computer games! *Both MJS*

HONEYBOURNE BRIDGE: The 1971 single-track steel span is seen in April 2009, looking south along the alignment of the former Cheltenham to Stratford main line towards Broadway. The road on the left-hand side is a new farmer's access road, constructed to enable an adjacent User Worked Crossing to be closed. The area to the right of the fence-line will hopefully one day see a single line of railway when the Gloucestershire Warwickshire heritage railway extends north from Broadway to the island platform at Honeybourne. In the distance, along the line of the old Cheltenham line formation, can be seen a small girder bridge, which carries the Honeybourne to Mickleton road over the old Cheltenham line. Immediately beyond this bridge was the location of Honeybourne West Loop signal box. The actual junction, however, was almost underneath the bridge in the foreground, and the right-hand abutment walls can be seen to be at a shallower angle to accommodate the diverging double track that formerly led up to Honeybourne North Loop Junction and the station. The formation of that chord is now partially underneath the old Civil Engineers tip, and will require partial excavation or an amended alignment to bring the steam railway back up to Honeybourne station.

By 13 September 2010 preparations to take the new double-track span are under way, with steel reinforcing rods being placed in position in front of the original brick abutments, while the first sections of shuttering for the concrete are being erected on the right. Amidst this frenzy of civil engineering equipment and activity it is perhaps difficult to picture the important double-track junction that once existed at this location.

A few months later, on 9 April 2011, the view is widened to show the new bridge and its abutments in all their glory! Double track is now in place again on the bridge, although the new up line is not yet connected and trains will continue to use a single set of rails until August. The fence-line and the farmer's access route have been restored under the new span and 'passive provision' has been left by Network Rail for the eventual restoration of a single line by the Gloucestershire Warwickshire Railway back to Honeybourne station. The heritage line was given permission to install a panel of track on the future formation as an 'indication of future intent', and this was laid in February 2011. *Tim Maddocks/MJS (2)*

HONEYBOURNE BRIDGE: On Thursday 30 September 2010, shortly before the start of the weekend blockade on the Friday night, a down **FGW HST** service passes over the old single-track bridge at Honeybourne and begins to slow for the station stop approximately half a mile away. The new concrete abutments can just be seen, waiting to take the new span in a couple of days' time.

On 9 April 2011 the scene is transformed, as **FGW** unit No 166216 passes over the new structure with another down service. The new up line is laid but not yet in use; it will not be connected at either end until a major engineering blockade in August 2011. For the technically minded, most of the new double line installed on the **OWW** route during 2011 is continuously welded **CEN56 (kg/m)** flat-bottom rail on **G44** concrete sleepers with Pandrol Fast-Clip clips and housings. The ballast depth is a minimum of 200mm. *Both MJS*

HONEYBOURNE BRIDGE: Seen on the afternoon of Saturday 2 October 2010, the new bridge deck is in place, and a waterproof membrane and 'bottom ballast' have already been installed. There is still some formation work to be completed on either side of the new span, and the reinstatement of the track would follow later that night.

Looking west from the same vantage point on 29 March 2011, the railway has reopened to traffic, with all service trains still using the left-hand track as a single line controlled by the electric token system between Moreton-in-Marsh and Evesham. The new order has already appeared, however, with the yet-to-be-commissioned up line on the right, which already has some shine on the rails due to the passage of road-rail machines. *MJS/Lee Moyle*

MICKLETON is approximately 2 miles east of Honeybourne, and on 21 April 2009 a **FGW HST** approaches the overbridge there at speed with an up working to London Paddington. The original cable troughing route to the left of the train will need to be moved prior to the installation of the second track, and a new route has already been laid in on the right-hand side. This area had also benefited from a major programme of cutting back the lineside vegetation inside the railway boundary fence, which was no doubt of great benefit to the engineers working on the redoubling project.

We now move to 2 October 2010, during the major weekend possession for the bridgeworks at Honeybourne and Evesham. Amey Colas has taken the opportunity of a total line blockage for the whole weekend to undertake further **PW** preparation works for the forthcoming installation of the second track, which would commence on mid-week nights later in the year, continuing on that basis without any significant interruption to train services until May 2011. A tracked digger sits on top of a supply of new ballast, and the limits of this particular engineering worksite can be seen in the distance behind the road/rail vehicle, in the form of a marker board; this carries two yellow lamps, one above the other, denoting the exit from the site. In order for any rail vehicles to pass this board, the Engineering Supervisor (**ES**) in charge of the site must obtain the permission of the Person In Charge of the Possession (**PICOP**). The reverse side of the marker board features two red lights, also vertically mounted, which denote that permission for a rail vehicle to enter the worksite must be obtained by the **PICOP** from the **ES**.
Tim Maddocks/MJS

MICKLETON: Just over two weeks later, on 17 October 2010, a down **FGW HST** service to Worcester speeds past the same site, with power car No 43151 at the rear. In just over 10 months the same service will be using the new down line at this point!

The three previous views seem to doubt the possibility of a second track, but here it is. On 14 June 2011 the layout is already looking as though it had been ever thus, as No 166207 heads towards Honeybourne forming the 0921 Paddington-Worcester Foregate Street service. Nature has very quickly recolonised both sides of the trackbed. *Both MJS*

MICKLETON: Turning through 180 degrees, we see the HST from the opposite page approaching the Mickleton overbridge. The distant hills form the natural barrier through which Campden Tunnel was driven. During the construction of the route in 1851 a dispute with one contractor caused the company to bring in additional labour. This was not to the liking of the original contractor's men, with the result that fisticuffs and general disarray developed between the rival gangs in the vicinity of the tunnel, an event now known as 'The Battle of Mickleton'. The local magistrate, soldiers and even Brunel himself got involved before the dispute was settled!

Again we see No 166207 from the opposite page, approaching the vantage point of the road overbridge. The sentinel tree still stands proudly. *Both MJS*

CHIPPING CAMPDEN BANK: 'Castle' 4-6-0 No 7000 *Viscount Portal* climbs Chipping Campden bank, a quarter of a mile west of Campden Tunnel, on Whit Monday, 3 June 1963, with the 12.05pm Hereford-Paddington express. The coaching stock is a rake of Mark 1 vehicles in a mixture of maroon and chocolate and cream liveries. This location is close to the western portal of the tunnel, near a road overbridge known as 'Ninevah Road', where a temporary access point for plant, machinery and staff was constructed in an adjacent field during the August 2009 blockade. It was during this six-week possession that the existing single line through Campden Tunnel was relaid and slewed across to the up side, and a new down line installed.

In the second view Hawker-Siddeley 2,750hp Co-Co diesel No D1748 (later Class 47) is about to enter the tunnel with the 12.25pm Hereford-Paddington express on Saturday 26 June 1965.

Finally, looking in the other direction, No 7031 *Cromwell's Castle*, in rather grubby external condition, coasts down from the tunnel on Saturday 25 May 1963 with the 5.15pm Paddington-Hereford train (the 'Cathedrals Express'), again formed with a rake of mixed-liveried Mark 1 coaches. This location saw the double track restored in August 2011. *All Mike Mensing*

CAMPDEN TUNNEL: In gloriously attractive surroundings, a Swindon three-car 'Cross-Country' DMU set emerges from Campden Tunnel on Saturday 15 June 1963, heading west as the 1.25pm Kingham-Worcester Shrub Hill local service.

In the opposite direction, climbing up to Campden Tunnel on the same day, 'Castle' Class 4-6-0 No 7005 *Sir Edward Elgar* heads the 12.05pm Hereford to Paddington express. The delightful area remains heavily wooded to this day. *Both Mike Mensing*

CAMPDEN TUNNEL: Ex-GWR 2-8-0 No 3859 climbs towards the tunnel with an up freight at 11.57am on Saturday 15 June 1963, with 0-6-0 'Collett Goods' No 2222 banking. The two leading wagons appear to be long-wheelbase flat wagons, possibly carrying sheet steel, although this is covered over with tarpaulins. The days of heavy freight trains requiring banking have long gone from the OWW route; indeed, any kind of freight traffic is currently sparse between Honeybourne and Wolvercot Junction, Oxford, although the current redoubling project should increase line capacity to the point where some resurgence in traffic is possible.

Shortly afterwards, at 12.13pm, Bo-Bo diesel-electric No D6508 (later Class 33 in the TOPS era) approaches the tunnel with an up fitted freight consisting of Esso oil tankers. The train is probably returning empty tank wagons from the Midlands to Fawley, a traffic frequently worked by one (or a pair) of this class of locomotive following their introduction. Note that this loco has not yet acquired the high-visibility yellow ends that would later become mandatory on all traction units on **BR**. Some of the Class 33 diesel fleet actually went straight from the all-over green livery to **BR** 'Corporate Blue' with full yellow ends, thus missing the 'small yellow warning panel' phase that others of the fleet carried with their earlier green livery. *Both Mike Mensing*

CAMPDEN TUNNEL: Back on the ground, this is the view from the western portal of the tunnel on 20 August 2009, looking towards Honeybourne and Worcester. Some examples of the heavy plant used during the blockade carry out their last few tasks at this end of the tunnel, prior to the hand-back of the possession and the reopening of the railway to normal operation.

Travelling to the other end on the same day, this is the view from inside the eastern portal looking towards Oxford. The new up line is virtually ready for use, although it will continue to serve as the sole running line between Evesham and Moreton-in-Marsh for another two years, until the major blockade in August 2011. The new down line has been installed through the tunnel, the rail ends just poking out into the daylight at either end. The rest of the new down line on either side of the tunnel will be installed in the five months between December 2010 and May 2011, but the fact that the engineers didn't have to lay track through the confines of the tunnel itself during their programme of mid-week night possessions was a major logistical benefit. *Both Tim Maddocks*

CAMPDEN TUNNEL: 'Hymek' B-B diesel-hydraulic No D7052 exits the tunnel at the Oxford end and runs down the gradient towards Chipping Campden station with the 5.26pm Worcester to Paddington express on Saturday 18 June 1966. The Distant signal is off and the light load is surely not taxing the locomotive.

Looking towards Worcester on 28 July 2009, the effect of the re-grading work on the cutting side

is more apparent. The browny-grey of the earthworks is in stark contrast to the verdant green of the woodland above the tunnel! On this date the single running line had been cut back to a point just behind where the photographer was standing. *Mike Mensing/Tim Maddocks*

CAMPDEN TUNNEL: On 26 July 2009 Amey Colas engineers are busy working on the new trackside drains and other formation works on the approach to the tunnel's eastern portal. Civil engineers are busy in the background re-grading the slope of the cutting side, to ensure that the redoubled railway here doesn't suffer from the problems of bank slips or poor drainage. A new GSM-R mast and equipment room has already been installed at the side of the trackbed, although it had not been commissioned when this photograph was taken.

This view was taken during the major six-week blockade of the OWW route, to permit major 'enabling' works for the redoubling project to be completed. While the main job during this time was the complete relaying of the existing single line through the tunnel, elsewhere Amey S&T engineers were busy on a programme of moving lineside equipment cabinets and other associated equipment clear of the path of the new double track. Over the years British Rail had slewed the remaining single line across to the centre of the formation, to allow higher speeds or a smoother ride. While this made sense at the time, it obviously needed to be 'undone' for the line to be redoubled.

We return to the same location a few weeks later on 20 August 2009, and what a difference! The formation and cutting works are complete and smart new concrete-sleepered track has been laid, ballasted and tamped, ready for traffic a few days later. The local PW maintenance team will be glad of the new 'cess' walkway provided on the right-hand side. New drainage catch-pits have been installed – a reminder that one of the first major jobs following removal of the old track was to excavate and install a new, more efficient drainage system through the tunnel. The cutting sides have been seeded with a fast-growing type of grass, the seeds of which are green in colour – the effect is just as if someone had scattered dyed sawdust on model railway scenery! A few weeks after this picture was taken, however, new grass was firmly established on the new earthworks, so the seed 'did what it said on the tin'! *Both Tim Maddocks*

CHIPPING CAMPDEN station, with its wooden structures, is still open in August 1962 as No 7004 *Eastnor Castle* steams through with a down working to Hereford from Paddington. Note the height and architecturally individual style of the chimney on the main station building – presumably to more adequately draw smoke from the waiting room fireplace – and the attachment of telegraph insulators to it, which are probably linked to the 'You may telephone from here' notice affixed to the building. The up platform has just a rudimentary waiting shelter, but beyond there is a substantial goods shed just visible above the train.

The same view at 1138 on 19 June 2011, 45 years after the station's closure, shows a total transformation as No 43151 heads the 0935 Paddington-Hereford service past the site. That work has been progressing on redoubling at this point and across the level crossing, to the photographer's right, can be seen with the second track just visible alongside the HST power car. Just above this new track, the white roof of a lorry in a lineside compound indicates the location of the erstwhile goods shed. The crossing, with lifting barriers, is monitored from Moreton-in-Marsh by CCTV, and remained controlled in this way after the line was redoubled in August 2011, although the equipment was renewed and repositioned as necessary to allow for the reinstatement of the double track. *M. L. Boakes, MJS collection/MJS*

CHIPPING CAMPDEN: In the days of double track, 'Hymek' B-B No D7040 passes Chipping Campden station on 12 October 1963 with a Worcester-Paddington train. These handsome diesel-hydraulics shared the OWW line express workings with steam at this time, although not for much longer. They put in many competent performances on the line until withdrawal and replacement by diesel-electric power. Note the characterful old wooden goods shed on the left, which by now appears to be largely disused. The signal box, which controlled the level crossing and station area, can just be glimpsed through the open archway of the goods shed. The station opened in June 1853 and was initially called 'Mickleton', but the name was subsequently changed to Chipping Campden.

The station closed on 3 January 1966, and the tall poplar trees behind the 'Hymek'-hauled train have disappeared during the 43 years between these views, as we look towards the site of the station on 4 September 2006. The level crossing, now controlled by CCTV from Moreton-in-Marsh signal box, and the red aspect of its protecting signal MM102 can just be seen in the distance. When it was opened Chipping Campden station was around a mile from the town, although the same cannot be said today, as new developments have brought the built-up area much closer to the railway. Although not part of the current investment project, Network Rail will leave 'passive provision' for a possible reopened station here in the future. The town itself is a delightful architectural gem and deservedly popular with visitors to the Cotswolds. *Millbrook House/MJS*

CHIPPING CAMPDEN: Here is No 7005 *Sir Edward Elgar* again, making light work of the 10-coach train, totalling approximately 340 tons, as it departs from Chipping Campden station on Saturday 25 May 1963 with the 2.05pm Hereford to Paddington express. The line was level through the station, but this train will climb at 1 in 151 then 1 in 184 to the summit of the route at Moreton-in-Marsh.

We now 'fast forward' some 47 years to find the scene significantly changed. Three-car FGW 'Turbo' unit No 166204 passes the site of the station as the 1107 Great Malvern to Paddington service on 17 October 2010. The front of the unit is about to pass a milepost that tells us that we are 96¾ miles from Paddington. Pallets of concrete cable troughing units have been delivered to site, but there is little else to tell us that the line through here is about to be redoubled. All this would change and by April 2011 the new down line would be installed, waiting to be connected up and opened to traffic the following August.

We are now back with double tracks and in 'express' mode, with No 43123 at one end of the 1022 Paddington-Hereford service on Tuesday 14 June 2011. As at Mickleton, the 'imposition' of the second track onto nature has been so skilfully done that there is no join! Note the proliferation of cars parked in the wayside field, presumably at some event.
Mike Mensing/MJS (2)

CHIPPING CAMPDEN: No 2885, one of the Churchward 2-8-0 heavy freight locos that were often rostered over the OWW in the days of steam heads towards Chipping Campden with a down partly fitted freight at precisely 4.11pm on Saturday 25 May 1963. It will shortly pass the goods yard and the site of the former connection to the Chipping Campden Coal, Coke & Lighting Company's private siding.

On 14 June 2011 the new down track is in place as No 43160 heads north-west with the 1022 Paddington-Hereford express. The growth of the lineside trees to the right has meant that the present view is slightly to the left of the earlier shot, but the lineside hut is still in the picture, though only just visible amongst the greenery. Note the new trunking to the left of the lines.
Mike Mensing/MJS

ASTON MAGNA: No 47502 rounds the curve at Aston Magna on 8 May 1982 with an up express. Despite the proximity of the railway to the village at this point, no station was ever provided here, the nearest previously being Blockley or Moreton-in-Marsh (some 2 miles to the south).

On a cold 7 February 2011, the second, telephoto, view of the same curve emphasises the preparations that are taking place for the redoubling of the line between Evesham and Moreton-in-Marsh. The formation has been prepared for the new up line, with new rails already laid out in the 'four-foot' of the existing line. A new concrete troughing route is also ready to receive its signalling cables. Standing sentinel over the scene is one of Network Rail's new GSM-R radio masts, which will replace the existing 'Cab Secure Radio System' on the OWW route in the near future. This will ensure an enhanced level of secure radio communications between train drivers and controlling signal boxes.

On Tuesday 14 June 2011 the new track is in, ballasted and ready for use at the end of the final works in August. No 166207 forms the 1206 Worcester Foregate Street-Paddington roster as it rounds the curve and passes the work to create a concrete base and fencing for a lineside cabinet. *John Whitehouse/Tim Maddocks/MJS*

ASTON MAGNA: '22XX' 0-6-0 No 2246 trundles past Aston Magna on Saturday 25 May 1963 with the 5.50pm Honeybourne to Moreton-in-Marsh shuttle, composed of what appears to be a Hawksworth Brake Composite coach. Having served at Stourbridge, Banbury and Didcot sheds among others during its career, the loco was moved to its final home, 85A (Worcester), in November 1960. Its demise came seven months after this view. *Mike Mensing*

DORN: Not a desirable state of affairs! Thought to have been caused by the wettest July in 50 years, a landslip occurred at Dorn, near Moreton-in-Marsh, in July 1988, where a 40-foot-high embankment gave way following heavy rain. The result is seen on 26 July, with a 5-foot-deep and 20-foot-long hole that needed 4,000 tons of stone to make good. Repairs cost £100,000 at the time, and took 2½ weeks. The presence of the 5mph emergency speed restriction signs indicates that some kind of a problem was already being monitored here, because the track as depicted in this photograph is definitely not fit for the passage of trains, even at that low speed! *Mike Mensing*

MORETON-IN-MARSH is the highest point on the OWW route, the station here having been opened on 4 June 1853. On 7 July 1978 No 50012 *Benbow* accelerates away from the Moreton-in-Marsh stop with the 1700 Paddington to Hereford service. The leading vehicle is a Mark I Full Brake, recalling the days when this kind of accommodation was common on passenger trains. The line at this location had only been single track for seven years, and the sleeper indentations of the former up line are still apparent to the right of the remaining track.

Seen from the same viewpoint on 4 October 2010, the 1022 Paddington to Hereford service departs from Moreton-in-Marsh towards Evesham. This was the Monday following the major weekend possession, when the bridge at Honeybourne was replaced and major relining works carried out on the River Avon bridge east of Evesham. Pallets of new concrete troughing sections have been delivered to site and there is evidence of the signalling cables having been worked on in the down 'cess'. This section of the (then) single line was relaid with new flat-bottom rail and steel sleepers during the six-week blockade in August 2009. New rails have also been delivered to site and are laid out in the 'four-foot' of the running line, in preparation for the installation of the new up line, which would commence in the spring of 2011.

With increasing usage of and heavy lorries over the narrow road bridge, the third view is from a safer vantage point, slightly to the left. With the new track to the right on 6 June 2011, No 166211 is approaching the station as the 0954 Great Malvern-Paddington service. Again the new layout contrasts with the very limited accommodation that was apparent in the days of the single line. *Mike Mensing/ MJS (2)*

MORETON-IN-MARSH:
Returning to 7 July 1978, we turn the camera through 180 degrees and see **No 50012** *Benbow* again as it departs from the down platform at **Moreton-in-Marsh.** The rest of the train appears to be formed of **Mark 2 coaching stock.** The driver will now be in possession of the single-line electric token, which will give him authority to occupy the section as far as Evesham, some 12 miles away. Note the cable troughing route, which snakes from the rear of the up platform along the formation of the old up line next to the train.

The road bridge at the north end of the station provides us with the same angle more than 32 years later on 4 October 2010, as a **FGW HST** headed by **No 43122** awaits the 'right away'. The line to Evesham is still single track and the general scene surrounding the track is little altered since 1978, with the exception of the inevitable vegetation. The former timber yard next to the station has now been redeveloped and careful observers will note that the station footbridge has been replaced by a more modern version with disabled access ramps in addition to stairs. *Mike Mensing/MJS*

MORETON-IN-MARSH:
On the night of Thursday 3 February 2011, Amey Colas PW staff are busy unloading concrete sleepers from an engineering train, as they get on with the vital job of laying in the new running line to the north of the station. With the exception of the Christmas holidays, engineering trains such as this ran over the OWW route almost every night from early December 2010 until May 2011, delivering ballast, sleepers and long welded rail for the redoubling project. Each overnight possession saw around 1,400 sleepers unloaded and laid out, the equivalent of around 800 metres of track. Before the new track can be laid, the formation of the old line must first be excavated and spoil removed – also by train. New 'bottom ballast' is then laid and bulldozed flat to the required geometry, following which the actual tracklaying can take place.

It's long after midnight now, on the morning of Friday 4 February, and the Amey Colas workers are keeping up the momentum of tracklaying as a track gang clips rail into place on new sleepers to form the new up line north of the station. *Both Phil Haigh*

MORETON-IN-MARSH: The passengers have long gone home as we look south from the previous photograph on the same night and see the extent of the 'head of steel' as it approaches the station. A road/rail vehicle awaits its next job in the distance. The new track in this picture will be connected up to the rest of the track layout in the big engineering blockade in August 2011, which will see double track extend from Gishbourne Farm User Worked Crossing, west of Evesham, right through to a point just east of Charlbury. The existing crossover at Moreton will be renewed in its current position, and will become the only crossover facility between Honeybourne and Charlbury. The north-end loop points seen in this photograph will be recovered at the same time.

The presence of the newly laid up line becomes clearer in daylight on Monday 7 March 2011, as a couple of S&T technicians adjust the loop points at the north end of the station. The scene is framed by the pleasant Cotswold stone overbridge, from which some of the earlier views were taken, and which will again span a double-track railway from August 2011. *Phil Haigh/MJS*

MORETON-IN-MARSH: No 47499 crosses sister loco No 47152 at Moreton-in-Marsh on 7 July 1978 as it brings the nine coaches of the 1845 Hereford to Paddington service into the station; the 1800 ex-Paddington, already running late, waits in the opposite platform. The driver of No 47499 will return the single-line token from Evesham to the signalman at the signal box, which stands at the London end of the up platform. When the signalman has sent 'Train Out of Section' to Evesham and restored the token to the machine, he will then obtain 'Line Clear' for the down train waiting in the opposite platform. Fortunately for the driver of that train, he won't have to walk all the way back to the signal box to collect the token, as there is a 'remote' token machine on the down platform, from where a token will be released by the signalman.

Nearly 19 years later, on 14 June 1997, the redevelopment next to the down platform is revealed as a supermarket. Two-car 'Thames Turbo' unit No 165125 must already have the token as it departs as the 0848 Paddington to Great Malvern service. Note the special paving slabs recently installed in the up platform, to enable those with impaired vision to recognise when they are close to the platform edge; the down platform has not yet been modified. *Mike Mensing/MJS*

MORETON-IN-MARSH: Returning once more to 7 July 1978, we see No 47152 bringing the late-running 1800 Paddington to Hereford service into Moreton-in-Marsh and running down to No 5 signal to await the arrival of the up train. The signal box is visible at the end of the up platform, with the double track to Ascott-under-Wychwood disappearing into the distance. Note the second siding adjacent to the up platform bay; these two roads originally formed part of the more complex station layout when Moreton was the junction for the Shipston-on-Stour branch, which closed to passengers on 8 July 1929, with goods traffic continuing until May 1960. The land beyond the old brick goods shed in the middle distance has already started to be redeveloped with new housing.

From a similar viewpoint, using the new footbridge, No 166212 arrives forming the 1421 Paddington to Great Malvern service on 16 April 2011. The station appears substantially unchanged since the 1978 view and, although more housing has since appeared in the background, the old brick goods shed still stands. Note the matching **GWR** station benches; that on the down platform has been painted in **FGW** blue, while the one on the up platform appears to be painted chocolate and cream! *Mike Mensing/MJS*

MORETON-IN-MARSH:
Three-car Class 117 DMU
set L406 carries the 1970s
'refurbished' livery of white
with a blue stripe on 5 August
1979 as it arrives with a
Great Malvern to Oxford
service. An old GWR platform
trolley serves as a seat on
the down platform. At this
stage the Parcels and Red
Star office was still open for
business, although it became a
pleasant station café following
privatisation and the cessation
of that kind of traffic on the
railway system.

Three decades later we see another unit, albeit a much more modern version. On Sunday 29 May 2011 No 165133 draws to a stand forming the 1455 Worcester Shrub Hill to Kingham stopping service; it is terminating at Kingham as this is the second day of the week-long possession of the line between Ascott-under-Wychwood and Charlbury, to complete the doubling of the line between these two points, including new track, platforms and signalling. The station is a mix of old and new, with, in the left foreground, an attempt at brightening the platform with privately cared-for flower beds. *John Acton, MJS collection/MJS*

MORETON-IN-MARSH: On an unrecorded date in 1982 the signalman returns to his box, having collected the token from the driver of set L420, forming an up all-stations stopping train from Worcester Shrub Hill to Oxford.

On Sunday 29 May 2011 we once again see the signalman making his return to his box, but this time wearing the de rigueur 'hi-vis' vest! The service is that already seen on the opposite page. The yellow signs adorning the lamp standards are directions for travellers going on to Oxford, who must join the coach waiting in the station car park, due to the blockade further down the line. The sidings in the left foreground and the ground signal will all be gone after work during the possession of August 2011. *John Whitehouse/MJS*

MORETON-IN-MARSH: On an unrecorded date in the 1980s Class 47 No 47619 passes the distinctive Great Western signal box and lower-quadrant signals on the approach to Moreton-in-Marsh. The land to the right of the train, including the brick goods shed, still appears to be in BR ownership and a PW van lurks in the back of the yard. The down siding appears to be in good fettle, although by this time is more likely to be used by the engineers rather than any revenue-earning freight traffic.

The privatisation era is getting into its stride on Sunday 1 March 1998 as No 43142, in Great Western Trains green and ivory livery, heads the 1036 Paddington to Hereford service into the station. The trailer coaches are still sporting the 'InterCity Executive' livery. The down siding is still in situ and used by the engineers for stabling tampers, but the land to the right has now been fenced off for use as a car park. A yellow PW 'workabus' is again parked in the yard! *John Whitehouse/Steve Widdowson*

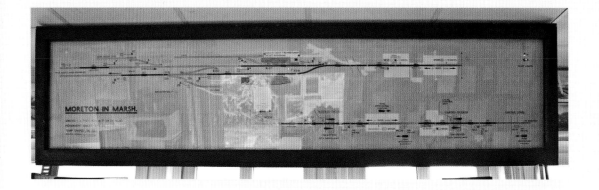

MORETON IN MARSH.

MORETON-IN-MARSH: Two views from the cab of a down train now follow, taken on 25 September 2002. On-track machines occupy both down and up sidings, the latter being the former Shipston-on-Stour bay platform, but the sidings will be removed as part of the track rationalisation and redoubling works in August 2011. Following the redoubling, on-track machines and any other similar vehicles will be catered for at Honeybourne where, as we have seen, the three remaining sidings in the old goods yard behind the station are being completely relaid for this purpose.

As our train moves closer to the station, we can see that the signal box has acquired some new double-glazed windows. While the improved energy-efficiency is undoubtedly welcomed by the signallers there, they do little for the aesthetic appearance of the structure! Fortunately a more enlightened attitude has since prevailed at a number of other ex-GWR locations, where the replacement windows have been provided with imitation GWR-style window bars, which in our view makes all the difference! Note that the original station footbridge is still in place. *Both Phil Marsh*

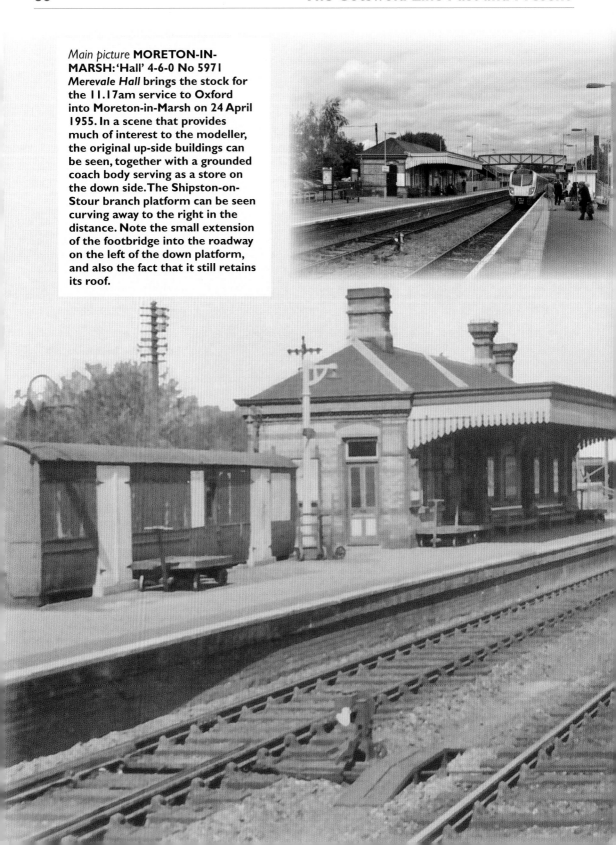

Main picture **MORETON-IN-MARSH:** 'Hall' 4-6-0 No 5971 *Merevale Hall* brings the stock for the 11.17am service to Oxford into Moreton-in-Marsh on 24 April 1955. In a scene that provides much of interest to the modeller, the original up-side buildings can be seen, together with a grounded coach body serving as a store on the down side. The Shipston-on-Stour branch platform can be seen curving away to the right in the distance. Note the small extension of the footbridge into the roadway on the left of the down platform, and also the fact that it still retains its roof.

Left: **On 4 September 2006 FGW five-car 'Adelante' unit No 180109 arrives with a Worcester Shrub Hill to Paddington service. Business appears good, and there are also passengers waiting for a down service. The old up-side building has long gone, but the down-side brick station building is still in use, although it has now lost its chimneys. A new, disabled-compliant station footbridge has been provided.**

Below: **The 150th Anniversary of the opening of the OWW line was celebrated at Moreton-in-Marsh on 4 June 2003 with an event organised by the CLPG. Thames Trains played its part by providing unit No 166212 as part of a display in the bay platform siding behind the signal box. This siding was to be removed in August 2011 as part of the track remodelling at Moreton during the redoubling.** *MJS collection/ MJS/Steve Widdowson*

MORETON-IN-MARSH: The up 'Cathedrals Express' (8.05am Hereford to Paddington) departs from Moreton-in-Marsh behind No 7013 *Bristol Castle* on 13 April 1963. The loco looks to be in reasonable condition and most of the original railway infrastructure in and around the station still seems to be intact. A 12-ton box van is being loaded at the small brick-built goods shed and the remains of the Shipston-on-Stour branch can be seen curving away to the right behind the signal box. Prominent in the foreground is a run of point rodding to various sets of points behind the photographer. *Bristol Castle* was built at Swindon in July 1948 but later swapped identities with No 4082 *Windsor Castle* before being withdrawn from Tyseley shed in March 1965.

The Down Home signal (now numbered MM4) still protrudes above an up train some 48 years later, as a very clean No 166205 accelerates away from the Moreton-in-Marsh stop, forming the 1432 Great Malvern to Paddington service on Saturday 16 April 2011. The rodding run still survives in the foreground, albeit slightly 'thinned out'. Another survivor is the brick

goods shed, which has been adapted to local business use. The two sidings in this modern-day view will be removed in August 2011, although the down refuge siding to the east of the station area will be retained for operational use. Although all three surviving mechanical signal boxes at Ascott-under-Wychwood, Moreton-in-Marsh and Evesham will remain following the redoubling project, only Moreton will retain its traditional signals; in fact, it will gain an additional semaphore signal, when an Up Starting signal will be provided to enable passenger trains to leave for Oxford from the down platform. *Hugh Ballantyne/MJS*

MORETON-IN-MARSH: Three-car set L588 (formed from two Class 119 carriages from a three-car set together with a Class 121 'bubble car') leaves Moreton-in-Marsh on 7 July 1978 as the 1741 Worcester Foregate Street to Oxford stopper. Another DMU stands in the down platform, waiting to depart towards Worcester. L588 will now travel along double track as far as Ascott-under-Wychwood. Note the surviving van-load freight traffic in the goods siding. Even as late as 1978 the former Shipston-on-Stour formation can be seen curving away to the right above the roof of the DMU.

The area next to the old branch-line formation seems to have seen some new buildings constructed as No 50048 *Dauntless* departs from Moreton-in-Marsh with the 16.15 Hereford to London Paddington express on 24 August 1986. The single-to-double connection can be seen immediately before the stone arch of the road bridge to the north of the platforms. Goods traffic seems to have disappeared from the down siding by this time.

By the date of the third view, 27 September 2003, the down goods siding is weed-choked and the former goods shed has lost its canopy, but all eyes are on No 4472 *Flying Scotsman* as she works an unidentified tour formed of the VSOE stock through Moreton-in-Marsh. The signal box had acquired its double glazing by this time. Note the tamper stabled in the former branch platform.
Mike Mensing/John Whitehouse/Steve Widdowson

MORETON-IN-MARSH: We are firmly in the BR 'Corporate Blue' era as three-car Class 117 DMU set L423 approaches Moreton-in-Marsh forming the 1649 service from Reading to Worcester on 7 July 1978. Note the allotments on the up side of the line, no doubt rented to railway staff. Some impressive telegraph poles remain a prominent feature of the railway landscape at this time. The down refuge siding was converted to a loop during the Second World War, but later reverted to siding status.

The previous view is now masked by trees, so this picture has been taken slightly to the left. No 166221 approaches Moreton on Saturday 16 April 2011, forming the 1321 service from Paddington to Great Malvern. The railway allotments have long gone, but the down refuge siding remains, albeit out of use in this view. It will be refettled prior to the big blockade in August 2011 and will be left in operational condition thereafter, the only remaining siding at Moreton-in-Marsh. *Mike Mensing/MJS*

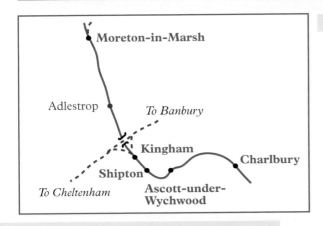

Moreton-in-Marsh

Adlestrop

To Banbury

Kingham

Charlbury

Shipton

Ascott-under-
Wychwood

To Cheltenham

ADLESTROP: No 7018 *Drysllwyn Castle* in full flight approaches Adlestrop station on 18 November 1961 with a Hereford-Paddington express. The station was opened in 1853 and closed on 3 January 1966. The photograph was taken from the road overbridge at the London end of the station that nowadays carries the A436 main road. Note the delightful wooden station building on the up platform. A smaller, matching wooden shelter is hidden by the trees on the down side, and the signal box is similarly hidden from view, this time behind the goods shed. A refuge siding was provided on the down side beyond the platform ends.

The passage of time and the works of man and nature have erased the station from the landscape and it is difficult to believe that there was ever a railway station at this location. FGW HST sets are the mainstay of the present-day express services, one of which approaches the site of Adlestrop station forming the 1243 Great Malvern-Paddington express on Saturday 16 April 2011. Both lines have been relaid since the 1961 view, the up line most recently, composed of steel sleepers and flat-bottom rail. *John Spencer Gilks/MJS*

ADLESTROP: The tall
Down Home signal is
'off' for Churchward
heavy freight 2-8-0 No 3805 as it heads west towards Adlestrop station with a long mixed
freight on 16 August 1958. Note the tall telegraph poles and their staying wires, a feature that
has long since disappeared from the railway scene in this age of the Internet and modern
telecommunications!

Looking at the same scene on 16 April 2011, it is possible to discern from the general
topography and the tree growth that this is the same location. No 43138 brings up the rear of
the 1243 Great Malvern-Paddington HST as it powers towards Oxford and Paddington. There
are no telegraph poles at Adlestrop, and no signals either, the block section now being from
Ascott-under-Wychwood to Moreton-in-Marsh. *MJS collection/MJS*

ADLESTROP: 'Castle' 4-6-0 No 7007 *Great Western* makes a fine sight as it storms south-east away from Adlestrop with the 1.15pm Paddington-Hereford express on 31 August 1962. Note the Up Distant signal for Kingham, which is showing 'off', thus informing the driver of train 1A22 that he has a clear road right through the station and beyond to the next block post. Kingham signal box was a mere 1 mile and 57 chains from Adlestrop. *Mike Mensing*

KINGHAM station is seen looking towards Worcester circa 1953. The station here was opened in 1855, some two years after the OWW route itself, and was initially called Chipping Norton Junction. Although the villages of Kingham and Bledington are equidistant from the station (both around half a mile away), the reference to Chipping Norton clearly reflected the latter town's higher status in the district. The branch lines to Chipping Norton itself and to Bourton-on-the-Water both opened in 1862, but the junction station did not become 'Kingham' until 1909. In this view, the left-hand arm on the distinctive junction bracket signal refers to the diverging chord to the Cheltenham line, the junction being immediately after the platform end. Out of view to the right are the two Chipping Norton and Banbury platforms, although the running line can just be seen in the right distance. The girder bridge in the distance carried a through connecting line, opened in 1906, enabling trains to run directly between Banbury and Cheltenham without having to reverse or call at Kingham. The best-known service booked over that

route was probably the 'South Wales Ports Express' from Newcastle to Barry, but this had ceased running by this time. The small loco shed – the second such structure at Kingham – was opened in June 1913, replacing an 1881 wooden structure that had closed in 1905, having been deemed to be a fire risk. The replacement shed itself closed in December 1962.

The fireman of No 92007 seems to have put some fresh coal on, as the 9F races through Kingham with the Esso oil tanks from Bromford Bridge to Fawley on 29

September 1962. The bracket signal on the right of the picture applied to the branch platforms. The passenger service beyond Chipping Norton to Banbury had already succumbed in 1951, and even the remaining trains to the former station would be withdrawn a few weeks after this photo was taken, in October 1962. The passenger service from Kingham to Cheltenham was also withdrawn at the same time, although freight traffic continued from Kingham to Bourton for a further two years. *Joe Moss, Roger Carpenter collection/Hugh Ballantyne*

KINGHAM: A Cheltenham-bound train waits in the branch platform on the far side of Kingham station in this view from the mid-1950s, looking towards Oxford. The running-in board reads 'KINGHAM – CHANGE FOR CHIPPING NORTON, BOURTON-ON-WATER & CHELTENHAM LINES'. Note the fine brick buildings on both platforms, although even then some of the valancing seems to be missing. A lattice footbridge graces the London end of the station. The journey to Cheltenham took approximately an hour, no doubt a contributing factor in the sad decline of this scenic route over the 'Cotswolds Top'. The island platform had been extended by some 115 feet in the 1880s and resulted in a change in levels, which can be seen here; the extension also resulted in the North signal box having to be moved further out from the station. One little-known fact about Kingham is that in Edwardian times the station master used to keep a pet pig!

On 27 October 1989 Kingham station presents a sobering illustration of the way that station infrastructure was 'rationalised' in the 1960s and 1970s. Gone are the characterful old brick buildings, demolished in 1975, that on the up platform having been replaced by a basic 'bus shelter'-type structure. Just visible on the right-hand side is the more modern, replacement brick station building. No canopy was provided when this was constructed in the 1970s, but at least the station remained staffed, enabling passengers to continue to purchase tickets and make train journey enquiries locally. The running-in board in this view is clearly not the one that originally stood in that position, but appears to be have been moved from another part of the station. The lattice footbridge still stands, albeit truncated at the former branch platforms.

The third photograph is the same view some 21 years later on 7 March 2011. The track has been relaid in the interim and the platforms resurfaced. The 1970s-era booking office is still staffed and business at this important Cotswolds railhead is good, the car park on the down side being frequently filled by commuters' cars each

morning. The old running-in board is also still extant and the whole station has benefited from a repaint in the FGW house colour of dark blue. The milepost reads 84¾ miles (from Paddington). A radio mast and relay room for the new GSM-R 'cab to shore' radio system stands in the up 'cess' just beyond the road overbridge. *MJS collection/MJS (2)*

KINGHAM: On Saturday 29 September 1962, during the final weeks of the passenger service to Chipping Norton, ex-GWR 'Large Prairie' No 4101 arrives at Kingham with the 4.25pm train from Chipping Norton. Modellers will note the configuration of the mass of point rodding from Kingham Station signal box that runs through the middle of the picture, and we are afforded a better view of the branch platform bracket signal. An unidentified BR Standard '78xxx' 2-6-0 stands in the shed in the background, possibly allocated to the Chipping Norton goods. The through line between Kingham East and West Junctions can be seen in the background, although this had closed as a through line on 23 September 1953, the signal boxes at either end closing on the same day.

Incredible as it may seem, this is the same view on 7 March 2011. The former island platform is now securely fenced and vegetation has taken hold of the former branch platform lines. *Hugh Ballantyne/MJS*

KINGHAM: A three-car Swindon 'Cross-Country' DMU (based at Tyseley) calls at Kingham on Saturday 2 September 1961, forming the 6.25pm Oxford to Moreton-in-Marsh stopper. Note that it also conveys two 10-foot-wheelbase box vans as 'tail traffic', something permitted in the operating regulations of the time. A platform barrow waits on the up main platform, well laden with parcels, for an Oxford-bound service. Note the dip in this platform, also visible in some of the earlier photos, and the different (brick) surface as compared with the stone slabs nearer the station buildings.

This 21st-century view sadly does not have the charm of yesteryear! On a dull 6 June 2011 HST power car No 43020 slows for the stop at the station at the head of the 0822 Paddington-Hereford express, running some 9 minutes late. The station house, on the right in the earlier view, still stands but is now masked by the tree growth. *Mike Mensing/ MJS*

KINGHAM: This fine view of the station was taken in 1962 from the road overbridge at the London end, with a Chipping Norton train in the branch platform. The scene abounds with items of interest to the modeller, such as the water crane on the up main platform, the Up Starting signal, different designs of platform lamps, and the neat white stones around the station flower beds. Visible to the right of the photo is the short extension to the station footbridge, which enabled passengers to gain direct access to an adjacent hotel.

On 16 April 2011 the present-day scene from the same viewpoint reveals that the footbridge has been truncated on the former island platform. The hotel next to the station is still in business, but prospective clients must now reach it via the main road bridge. It is also pleasing to note that there are still well-tended flower beds at Kingham. *MJS collection/ MJS*

KINGHAM: On 24 May 1955 'Dukedog' 4-4-0 No 9015 brings the Railway Enthusiasts' Club's 'South Midlander' rail tour into the branch platforms at Kingham. Even then it seems to have been 'de rigueur' for gricers to lean out of carriage windows! No 9015 remained in service until June 1960, when it was withdrawn from Machynlleth shed and scrapped in November at Swindon Works. Sister loco No 9017 is now the only example of this class to be preserved. While she is normally based on the Bluebell Railway, she has travelled to other preserved lines in recent years, even taking part in a splendid gala event on the Llangollen Railway, close to her former stamping ground on the Cambrian system.

The present-day view of the old branch platforms at Kingham was taken on 7 March 2011. While confirming the extent to which nature has reclaimed the disused portion of the station, it is pleasing to note the restored ex-**GWR** station seat still giving good service and the colourful flower beds, clearly someone's pride and joy! *Hugh Ballantyne/MJS*

KINGHAM: No 4142 arrives at Kingham with the 6.28pm train from Cheltenham Spa St James on Saturday 2 September 1961. The through service from Cheltenham via Stow-on-the-Wold would only last for another year, being withdrawn in October 1962, just two coaches sufficing for many trains during the latter years. Kingham's station footbridge had originally been provided with a covered roof, but this was deemed life-expired in the 1950s and was removed.
Mike Mensing

KINGHAM: No 7005 *Sir Edward Elgar* starts away from Kingham with the 2.05pm Hereford to Paddington express on 13 April 1963. The connections from the branch platforms can be seen to the right of the locomotive. The Langstone Arms Hotel, which for many years enjoyed a direct footbridge connection from the station, is just out of view to the right. *Hugh Ballantyne*

KINGHAM: No 7002 *Devizes Castle* approaches Kingham with the down 'Cathedrals Express' on Saturday 2 September 1961. The branch platform connections are clearer in this view, and a solitary box van stands in one of the up sidings. The very tall Down Home signal is no doubt configured in this manner for approach sighting purposes, possibly in connection with the overbridge in front of it. *Mike Mensing*

SHIPTON: Located just over 3 miles from Kingham, the station serving the village of Shipton-under-Wychwood is seen circa 1910 in this view looking towards Worcester. A down passenger train is just departing and goods traffic is looking healthy. Horse-power clearly still predominates on the local roads. With the popular Cotswold village of Burford some 5 miles to the south, the station

was known as 'Shipton for Burford' at one time. Chipping Norton was also close, being approximately 6 miles north of the station. On the left is Matthews' flour depot. Note the 1884 signal box, unusually set back some distance from the running line.

An unidentified FGW 'Adelante' Class 180 unit passes through Shipton station on 24 July 2005, on its way from Paddington to Worcester. The original platform buildings are long gone, but at least the station is still open for business. The line here (between Moreton and Ascott) was the only section to be left as double track in 1971, apart from the crossing loop at Evesham. The Matthews building still stands, thus readily identifying the modern scene with the previous view. *Lens of Sutton collection/MJS*

ASCOTT-UNDER-WYCHWOOD: The eight-day blockade of late May/early June 2011 saw the line between Charlbury and Ascott handed over the engineers, to complete the building of new second platforms at both locations and installing the remaining sections of track to go with these new facilities. On the northern approach to Ascott on Tuesday 31 May Colas-liveried No 66842 waits for its train of sleepers and ballast to be finally emptied before it leaves and makes its way to its initial destination at Bescot.

Meanwhile, to the rear of that train, work begins on cutting up the rails and point levers on what was the erstwhile crossover from double to single line, the oxyacetylene torch making light work of the task.

Yet further along the line, the station level crossing has been temporarily removed, as work is in place to prepare a bed for the new platform track. The arm of a road/rail machine frames No 66141 on another infrastructure train, while the ramp of a low-loader is down to off-load another on-track plant machine. Ascott's signal box stands to the right, overseeing it all. *All MJS*

ASCOTT-UNDER-WYCHWOOD: We jump back in time a little, to Saturday 8 January 2011, with 'Turbo' unit No 166201 approaching the station as the 1102 Worcester Shrub Hill-Paddington service, as seen from the signal box. The train is running through the double-to-single connection at 80 miles 38 chains at the maximum permitted speed of 40mph. With a ruling line speed in the up direction of 75mph from Moreton-in-Marsh to Ascott, and an increased line speed of 100mph forward to Wolvercot Junction, the reduction of speed at Ascott has long been an operational inconvenience. This will now be consigned to history when the redoubling project is completed, with double track extending right through from Evesham to Charlbury. Modellers will once again note the point rodding extending from the signal box; this, together with all remaining mechanical levers, will be removed from Ascott signal box during the May/June blockade, when a miniature push-button signalling panel will be installed to control the line from here to Charlbury and beyond.

At the same spot on Tuesday 14 June 2011, No 166204 heads in the opposite direction, operating as the 1421 Paddington to Moreton-in-Marsh service. No speed restriction remains, as the second track is well and truly in place to the right, opened to public passenger working just eight days earlier. *Both MJS*

ASCOTT-UNDER-WYCHWOOD: On Saturday 8 January 2011 clearance work has clearly started on the site of the new platform and track, but the lack of activity on this date has allowed the signaller to park his car next to the level crossing barriers. Note the original road surface and crossing barriers, which span the whole width of the road. Rail for the new up line has been placed in the 'four-foot' of the existing single line at this point.

Moving forward to 14 June 2011, the contractors are putting the finishing touches to the station, which has actually been open for business for just over a week. The contrast with the scene a mere five months previously is notable; the new up line is in place and the down line has also been relaid through the platform. The level crossing has been completely renewed as part of the project, with a new road surface and upgraded barriers – four in place of the original two. Note also the pleasing Cotswold stone finish to the new construction. *Both MJS*

ASCOTT-UNDER-WYCHWOOD: It is 0746 on Monday 6 June 2011 and the first of the **OWW** blockades has only finished some 3 hours previously. Thus it is Opening Day for the new double track between Ascott-under-Wychwood and Charlbury, as No 165121 approaches Ascott station with 2E92, the 0651 Worcester Foregate Street to Oxford service, the first (and currently the only) up stopping train to call. The 'T' ('Termination') board for one of the temporary speed restrictions associated with the new track can be seen on the left; this would be removed a couple of weeks after the possession, following consolidation of the track.

Shortly afterwards an official welcome party comprised of railway personnel, local dignitaries and guests prepares to board the train. Celebration was the order of the day, as this was the first train to call at the up platform at this station for 40 years, after a ceremonial 'ribbon-cutting'. *Both MJS*

ASCOTT-UNDER-WYCHWOOD: On 13 April 1963 No 7928 *Wolf Hall* runs through the station with an up working. Just over two weeks have elapsed since the Beeching Report was published on 27 March 1963, the effects of which would take a few more years to filter down to the OWW route. Modellers may wish to note the apparently differing painting styles on the station building and signal box, where a greater use of the cream colour on the former arguably gives a cleaner, brighter impression. That said, a mere colour scheme would not be enough to save the station building, which would eventually be demolished and replaced by a 'bus shelter'-type structure. The up platform was removed following the singling of the line from a point towards the rear of the train through to Wolvercot Junction. The up line and platform were replaced during the eight-day late-May 2011 blockade and fully commissioned on Tuesday 23 August 2011. The three ladies are backpackers from South Africa … how on earth did they end up here?

The second picture is a more recent (yet now historical!) view from the cab of a service on 25 September 2002. The signal box still stands and remains operational, even seemingly retaining the same colour scheme as in 1963! Gone in this view are the original up line and platform.

Opened on 6 June 2011, just eight days before this view, the station is still receiving some last-minute attention, not least to the rear platform fencing. No 166217 roars through non-stop on 14 June forming the 1435 Great Malvern-Paddington service, here some 17 minutes late. *Hugh Ballantyne/Phil Marsh/MJS*

ASCOTT-UNDER-WYCHWOOD: Firmly in the post-singling era, yet prior to the removal of the last remaining siding at Ascott, No 47512 powers through the station en route to Oxford and London Paddington on 14 May 1981. This period marked the beginning of the resurgence of the OWW route, with Honeybourne station reopening a week later on the 22nd. The siding at Ascott would be removed in due course and the attractive old wooden station building has already disappeared. The signal box remains in the background, controlling the level crossing and the single-to-double connection immediately beyond.

Below left: **A souvenir of the first train on the reopened line, stopped especially to let guests alight!**

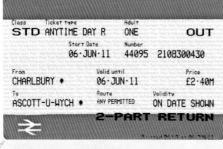

By 14 June 2011 the station has reopened with a new second platform and with the provision, for the first time, of a (admittedly rudimentary) car park. The sidings have long gone and the down platform has been lengthened and fenced. *John Acton, MJS collection/MJS*

CHARLBURY: In this early-1980s scene, refurbished Class 50 No 50022 *Anson* draws into the station with a Paddington to Worcester Shrub Hill express. The typical Brunellian 'chalet'-style station building, dating back to 1853 when the station was opened by the OWW (later absorbed into the GWR), was fortunately saved from demolition many years ago and is still carrying out its intended function, even retaining its open fireplaces! In this view, the remaining platform has not yet been extended towards Worcester, necessitating careful management of passengers joining and alighting from trains during that period. A new-looking cable troughing route has been installed in the trackbed of the former down line and all trace of the down platform has been erased. A wooden goods shed, similar to other structures on the OWW route, used to stand on the up side of the line beyond the station, but there is no trace of it in this picture because part of the area had already been turned into a station car park by this time.

The effects of the Cotswold Line redoubling project are obvious in the second view, from Monday 7 March 2011. Track is in place alongside the new platform, which is rapidly taking shape, as No 166210 enters the station as the 0921 Paddington to Worcester Foregate Street service. The railway curves away to the right towards Oxford, crossing the River Evenlode out of shot. The new double-to-single connection – with 'NR60 G 33.5' specification, an inclined

design on concrete bearers – will be installed to the east of the station, with higher-speed turnouts improving journey times. The improved layout will be controlled from a new mini signalling control panel in Ascott-under-Wychwood signal box. The redoubling project is taking advantage of engineering access to also install a new signalled 'turn-back' facility here, enabling terminating down trains to be signalled off the Oxford single line directly into the up platform, from which they can return to Oxford. This will be of great benefit, as otherwise trains would need to travel through to Moreton-in-Marsh to reverse.

Sunday 29 June 2011 saw the installation of a new footbridge to link to the new Platform 1. Later in the day the new platform is approaching the final stages of construction, while on the left workers concentrate on building a walkway to the bridge from the station car park. This now masks the previous views, much to the irritation of photographers. *John Whitehouse/MJS (2)*

CHARLBURY: These three views show the new footbridge from the ground on 29 May 2011. In the first, the main span is eased into position, with a section of the up-side pedestrian ramp seen to the right. Note the stout single columns that support each side of the structure. The new down platform can be seen in the background. Great care has been taken to ensure that the new works blend in with the existing surroundings, as evidenced by the quantities of Cotswold-coloured stone being used.

Two hours later real progress is being made, with the new footbridge waiting for the DDA ramps to be fitted. A sub-surface of tarmac has already been laid on the new down platform, which will receive a top layer, and a fence will be provided between the platform and the area under the ramps of the new footbridge.

Just 20 minutes later on this Day 2 of the first major OWW blockade, the first of the down-side pedestrian ramps is already in position and the second section is being lowered into position. A road-rail machine awaits a passage through the new platform line, once the crane activity has been completed. Following discussions between Network Rail, FGW and local stakeholders, it was agreed that the new footbridge would be finished in 'heritage' GWR light and dark stone, to match the existing colour scheme at the station. *All MJS*

CHARLBURY: On 15 May 1982, the last day of the Winter timetable and the last day of loco-haulage, enthusiastic gricers wave their curious 'salute' from the windows of the Full Brake as No 50033 *Glorious* leaves Charlbury, still with its short platform, bearing a 'Cathedrals Express' headboard, a throwback to the days when 'Castles' were the staple motive power on the expresses. The cable troughing route on the trackbed of the former down line would eventually be repositioned during the redoubling preparatory works.

The level of transformation, both over recent years with the lengthening of the up platform and with the latest redoubling project works and reinstatement of the down line and platform, is plain to see as No 43041 brings up the rear of the 1314 Hereford-Paddington service on Tuesday 14 June 2011. Note the retention of an original-style running-in board, with attendant garden, gracing the up platform. *John Whitehouse/MJS*

CHARLBURY: Looking back towards Moreton-in-Marsh and Worcester, not many passengers await the arrival of Class 50 No 50007 *Hercules* on 15 May 1982, heading an unidentified working to Paddington, framed by the attractive three-arch brick road bridge. The platform retains its original, short length at this end. Note the white-painted brickwork on the bridge, a common practice to assist train drivers to see semaphore signals. The curved arches over the doors and windows of the station building, unusual in a wooden structure, add a touch of refinement and mirror similar stone or brick buildings elsewhere on the GWR system.

The white patch on the bridge has survived the passage of time as No 166208 enters Charlbury as the 1008 Worcester Shrub Hill-Paddington service on 7 March 2011, to the delight of the waiting passengers, their pleasure no doubt increased at the sight of the redoubling works proceeding opposite them! A new 'fixed red' colour light signal will be provided to the west of the station, facing Oxford, to enable down trains to terminate in the up platform and start back towards Oxford. All new signals at Charlbury will be modern colour lights, of course, so the old white patch on the overbridge will no longer be needed! *John Whitehouse/MJS*

CHARLBURY: The first 'past' picture was taken as recently as 8 January 2011 and shows the preparations for the second track at Charlbury. The old down-line formation was excavated to a depth of 250mm, and new bottom ballast laid in and bulldozed flat, ready to take the new track. All this work was done during overnight mid-week possessions, typically from 2140 to 0500. This meant that the last trains over the OWW route were replaced by buses, in agreement with First Great Western. While admittedly an inconvenience for those who had to change to road transport, this method of construction avoided the need for more prolonged complete line blockages and enabled the vast majority of passenger trains to continue to run normally while the redoubling works were progressing.

A mere two months have passed, the new down line is already in place and work has started on the new platform. On 7 March 2011 the temporary fencing allows work by the contractors to continue safely while trains are running on the adjacent line.

A week after reopening, the weather smiles on the completed structures. On a warm and sunny 14 June 2011, celebration bunting has been taken down and the station slips into routine mode. The new facility, with a waiting shelter, new footbridge and small garden feature, certainly presents a pleasing aspect to the traveller.
All MJS

CHARLBURY: Infrastructure work continues on our railways regardless of weather conditions, unless they are exceptional. Thus, on Monday 30 May 2011, four days into an eight-day blockade of the route between Charlbury and Ascott-under-Wychwood, workers, observers – and even photographers – braved the decidedly unfriendly damp conditions as they went about their business. At precisely 0818, No 66019, with a track recovery train from Hinksey yard, Oxford, becomes the first train into a second platform at Charlbury for 40 years.

At 0714 just seven days later, the new Platform I receives its first passenger train for 40 years. Seen from the new footbridge, No 166207 slows for its milestone stop as the 0548 Paddington-Great Malvern service on 6 June, with a knot of dignitaries and invited guests celebrating its arrival, alongside the new fencing, waiting shelter and bunting. *David Northey/MJS*

CHARLBURY: This was the scene on Sunday 29 May 2011 at the site of what would become 'Charlbury Junction' in official parlance. We are just over a quarter of a mile to the east of Charlbury, looking west towards the station. The single line that had been in situ since 1971 had been removed by the engineers a few hours earlier and work is now well under way to prepare the trackbed for the new single-to-double connection. The approximate alignment has been marked with yellow paint on top of the newly laid 'bottom ballast', which has undoubtedly been compacted with the aid of the 'triple whacker' stabled on the left of the picture.

Only a day later, and from the same viewpoint, we can see that the new switch and crossing has been laid in and is awaiting final adjustments, ballasting and tamping. Charlbury station is just out of sight around the bend. Although the main elements of the PW work appear almost complete in this photograph, they would be followed by signal and telegraph works, including connections and comprehensive testing. The new pointwork is designed for 75mph, in stark contrast to the former 40mph double-to-single connection at Ascott-under-Wychwood. *Both MJS*

CHARLBURY: While the work was proceeding on the new single-to-double turnout at the eastern end of Charlbury station, No 66043 stood a few hundred yards further to the east, waiting to bring its Autoballaster train into the worksite to deliver its load of fresh ballast. At 1734 on the afternoon of 30 May 2011 the train enjoys a few rays of sunshine, very welcome after a day of sometimes heavy rain. *MJS*

CHARLBURY: Any work on our railways these days has to take into account the flora and fauna on and around the site. One such consideration on this project was the presence of Roman snails, a species protected under the Wildlife & Countryside Act 1981. The wet weather of 30 May 2011 saw them out in force and your photographer had to tread carefully as he prepared to capture the shot of the Autoballaster, recording one specimen for posterity. *MJS*

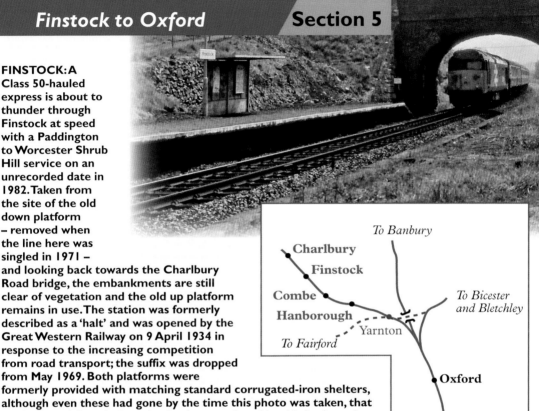

FINSTOCK: A Class 50-hauled express is about to thunder through Finstock at speed with a Paddington to Worcester Shrub Hill service on an unrecorded date in 1982. Taken from the site of the old down platform – removed when the line here was singled in 1971 – and looking back towards the Charlbury Road bridge, the embankments are still clear of vegetation and the old up platform remains in use. The station was formerly described as a 'halt' and was opened by the Great Western Railway on 9 April 1934 in response to the increasing competition from road transport; the suffix was dropped from May 1969. Both platforms were formerly provided with matching standard corrugated-iron shelters, although even these had gone by the time this photo was taken, that on the remaining platform having been replaced by this basic, rather spartan structure.

Yes, this is the same place, but the active platform has changed sides! On Saturday 16 April 2011 No 166209 speeds through non-stop as the 0943 Great Malvern-Paddington duty. Note how the newer platform has been constructed over the trackbed of the former down line, following the slewing of the single line through the centre of the brick arch. Modern signage helps would-be travellers orientate themselves, and a new 'Help Point' has recently been installed. These are modern and well specified, using digital technology, and have been provided at many rural, unstaffed stations across the First Great Western franchise area, providing a significant improvement in the quality of train information that has been welcomed by passengers. *John Whitehouse/MJS*

FINSTOCK: No D7009 enters Finstock station on Good Friday, 16 May 1965, with 1A36, the 10.35am Hereford to Paddington express. The original condition of the halt can clearly be seen, together with the very rural nature of the surroundings.

On 18 September 1994 No 47714, in 'Res' Parcels Sector livery, passes Finstock with a Wolverhampton-Poole diversionary train. Despite having previously expended money on realigning the track and providing a new platform, a closure notice had already been posted. On 18 May 1994 the following legend had been scrawled on the metal panels of the waiting shelter with a marker pen by persons unknown: 'OK we know graffiti is vandalism. Shutting down stations is even worse vandalism!' In June 1994 the Cotswolds Line Promotion Group organised a ramble ending at Finstock station. Fortunately closure did not happen, due to lobbying from the CLPG and others.

The future of the station seems more secure on 27 February 1999 as 'Thames Turbo' No 166218 passes non-stop forming the 1048 Paddington to Great Malvern service. Note the relatively new NSE-style paint scheme on the station as well as the 'Turbo' unit, which at that time was operated by Thames Trains. The observant may have also spotted that the shelter in this photo is none other than that in the earlier view with the Class 50, simply 'recycled' to the new platform! There are no plans currently to restore the double line between Charlbury and Wolvercot Junction, although this has been listed in the Network Rail (Western) Route Utilisation Strategy as a possible project for the future, should demand and traffic patterns justify it. *Mike Mensing/Steve Widdowson/MJS*

COMBE: No 50031 *Hood* passes Combe Halt on an unrecorded date with a down working. Introduced as No D431 in July 1968 (to BR's Stoke Division) and renumbered to 50031 in 1974, it was transferred to the Western Region in 1976, initially to Laira Depot, and was given its name in June 1978. It worked its last revenue-earning train under BR auspices (from Basingstoke to Exeter) on 15 July 1991 and was stored at Laira until formal withdrawal in August that same year, after which it was bought by The Fifty Fund in operational condition. Note the extremely rural nature of the location – Combe must be one of the smallest stations on the system.

From basically the same vantage point, a **FGW HST** set with power car No 43191 leading powers through Combe Halt at the full line speed of 100mph, heading towards Charlbury and Worcester. Although the hedgerow and field in the left foreground remain relatively clear, vegetation has grown up around and along the railway boundary in the intervening years. Although seemingly a casualty of the passage of time, the **PW** hut seen in the earlier picture is actually still there and can just be seen peeping out behind a small tree! *John Whitehouse/MJS*

COMBE: On 4 July 1993 No 47581 passes Combe Halt, working the 1005 (SuO) Poole to Glasgow train. This working in itself can now be considered an historical anachronism, in that FGW is the only train operator to work regular, timetabled passenger services over the OWW route. CrossCountry services are no longer even diverted via this line, other routes or bus substitution being preferred. At the time this photograph was taken, Combe Halt only had one booked stopping train each day (Mondays to Saturdays) – and that was only on a 'request stop' basis! The 'Res' Class 47 was also a rarity on a working such as this, as usually InterCity 47/8-type locos were allocated to this Sunday duty. Closure notices were posted for Finstock and Combe halts for 11 March 1994, but thankfully closure did not occur and both halts remain open to this day. This stretch of line is not currently part of the Cotswold Line redoubling project, although again it has been designated for possible future reinstatement should economic circumstances warrant it. *Steve Widdowson*

HANBOROUGH: Evidence of past glories could be seen at Handborough (original spelling) on 15 May 1982, with the long-abandoned down platform still very much present. The station boasts a rudimentary shelter for intending passengers as Class 50 No 50007 *Hercules* passes at the head of a Paddington to Worcester Shrub Hill train. This is a station with an interesting history, due to its proximity to Blenheim Palace, and was initially known as 'Handborough for Blenheim' when opened in 1853. Full goods facilities were provided and during the Second World War an additional siding was added for a Ministry of Food depot. When the connection to the LNWR's Bletchley line at Yarnton was installed, this was the first passenger station encountered from that direction, so the North Western advised its passengers to 'change at Handborough for Oxford'. The funeral train of Winston Churchill ran from Waterloo to Handborough, arriving there at 3.23pm on the afternoon of 30 January 1965; the great man was buried in nearby Bladon, near Woodstock. As with much of the OWW route, the line here was singled in 1971.

On 11 April 1991 No 155321 departs from Hanborough as the 0850 Oxford to Hereford service. The disused former down platform still survives amidst the vegetation, while the surviving one seems to have been recently resurfaced, and well-tended flower beds enhance the overall feel. The 'd' in the station name has also been dropped, the nameboards now reading 'Hanborough'.

In dull conditions on Saturday 16 April 2011, No 166214 slows for the stop at Hanborough as the 1032 Great Malvern to Paddington service. The station furniture has again changed and further tree growth, especially on the disused platform, gives the place a more enclosed feel. It is nonetheless still a well-tended station and is now well-patronised. The Oxford Bus Museum in the old station yard provides a welcome visitor attraction. In recent years, the station has been used as a temporary terminus during engineering works, as it is better suited than some to act as an interchange with replacement buses serving stations to the west. When this happens, 'Working by Pilotman' to and from 'Point of Obstruction' is introduced over the single line between Wolvercot and Hanborough, to enable trains to continue to run over the unaffected section of the OWW. *John Whitehouse/MJS (2)*

YARNTON: Again, the station here was isolated, but had importance as a junction. Although closed in 1962, platforms and signals still remain as '8750' pannier tank No 9773 arrives on 15 August 1965, bringing the LCGB 'Western Ranger' tour off the Witney and Fairford branch. This rail tour had started from Waterloo in London behind BR Standard Class 4

4-6-0 No 75066. A loco change then took place at Reading, where ex-GWR 2-8-0 No 3863 took charge. Then running via Swindon and back via Foxhall Junction to Radley, No 9773 substituted for the 2-8-0. The rail tour then ran to Abingdon, returned to Radley, then went via Oxford to Witney. Shortly after this photo was taken, No 9773 was taken off the train and 'Large Prairie' No 6126 attached for the next leg to Bicester and back to Oxford.

It's difficult to believe that this is the same location. With all traces of the former station now eradicated, No 43127 heads the 0843 Great Malvern to Paddington HST past the site on Saturday 16th April 2011.
Hugh Ballantyne/MJS

YARNTON: In happier days Yarnton signal box is seen here circa 1960, built higher than usual in order to give the signalman a better view of approaching trains; the style is reminiscent of the GWR signal boxes at Dawlish and Exeter Middle. The junction with the LNWR line to Bletchley was about half a mile east of the station; opened in 1854, the connection to the Oxford-Bletchley route was 1½ miles long, and at one point saw London Euston to Worcester trains running over it and past Yarnton Junction. The link was especially busy with freight services during the Second World War. *Lens of Sutton collection*

WOLVERCOT JUNCTION: No 50038 *Formidable* approaches the junction on 26 April 1987 with a Paddington to Hereford service. The former signal box stood on the down side of the line, but control of the area was subsequently taken over by Oxford Panel. The line from here to Oxford station and beyond was originally quadruple track, and even today up and down loops remain in use for the regulation of slower trains (the down loop does not come quite so close to the junction and is consequently not visible in this photograph). New in October 1968, as No D438, *Formidable* survived just one month short of two decades and was cut up at Vic Berry's scrapyard in Leicester in August 1989. *Steve Widdowson*

OXFORD NORTH JUNCTION: No 7002 *Devizes Castle*, with the second **BR** logo design on its tender, drifts slowly towards Oxford with an up parcels train, possibly from the **OWW** route, on 23 May 1963. To the right are the ex-**LNWR** tracks from Bicester to the former Oxford Rewley Road station, by this time only used for freight. Built in the last days of the GWR, No 7002 was a South Wales resident for the majority of its life, before moving east to Worcester shed in late December 1959. Withdrawal was on 13 April 1964.

The scene in the 21st century shows major change, with just the four tracks being common to both views. On 9 February 2011 No 66054 approaches Walton Well Bridge, immediately north of Oxford station, with an unidentified southbound Freightliner service. Note that the ex-LNWR trackbed is bare, but there has been talk of restoring track in view of the growth of passenger numbers over the Bicester line and the impending plans to run Oxford-Marylebone services over a new spur to the Chiltern line at Bicester. *Geoff King/Neil Beckley*

OXFORD: Shorn of its nameplates, 'Modified Hall' No 6967 *Willesley Hall* sits on Oxford shed on 15 August 1965, with an unidentified classmate and a BR Standard Class 4 for company. It was withdrawn at the end of the year, in line with the eradication of steam from the remaining BR(W) sheds. In the background 'Large Prairie' No 6126 passes with the LCGB 'Western Ranger' rail tour already seen at Yarnton, heading for the station. Oxford was a major location for locomotive changes on long-distance cross-country trains in the days of steam, with locos from all members of the former 'Big Four' being seen in and around the area. *Hugh Ballantyne*

OXFORD: 'Thames Turbo' No 166203 (cars 58124, 58603, 58103) stands in the down platform at Oxford on 17 June 1999 forming the 1248 Paddington to Great Malvern working. A Virgin HST sits in the up platform, no doubt on a working to the South Coast. Thames Trains existed as a franchised train operator from September 1996 until 31 March 2004 and operated mostly suburban services out of Paddington to destinations such as Slough, Reading and Oxford; it also operated longer-distance services to Newbury and Bedwyn, and over the OWW to Worcester and Hereford. From 1 April 2004 the franchise was acquired by First Group, which branded it as First Great Western Link and operated it alongside its existing First Great Western franchise. The two franchises were merged exactly two years later, together with the former Wessex Trains, to form the Greater Western franchise area, now operating as First Great Western. This merging of operators also fitted in with the policy of the then Strategic Rail Authority to have only one Train Operating Company predominating in any given London terminus. *MJS*

OXFORD: No 47631 arrives at Oxford on 23 April 1987 with one of the last loco-hauled 'Cathedrals Express' workings, the 0700 Hereford to Paddington, though without headboard by this stage. The two through lines to the left of the loco remain very busy to this day, with numerous through freight and other workings. The loco, too, survived at the time of writing, having been named *Ressaldar* in September 1993 and renumbered 47765 on 23 February 1994. *MJS*

OXFORD: An unidentified ex-GWR 'Large Prairie' 2-6-2T enters Oxford station from the north in the early 1960s with a long trip working bound for Hinksey Yard, just to the south of the station. The signal box is Oxford Station North, built in 1899. The lower brick portion of the box was strengthened during the Second World War against the effects of bomb blasts. The girders in the foreground take the railway over Sheepwash Channel, which was a connecting waterway between the River Thames and the Oxford Canal. Some of the buildings associated with the loco shed can just be seen on the left of the picture. *MJS collection*

OXFORD: Bay Platform 3 sees activity on Sunday 5 July 1998, as a pair of Class 156 units (Nos 156410 and 156402) are about to make a rare appearance in this part of the country working a Cotswold Line Promotion Group charter special to Barmouth. Note the 'Cotswold Cambrian Coast Express' headboard! Staff load catering items and boxes of other supplies essential for the trip prior to departure. *Steve Widdowson*

HONEYBOURNE 'Past & Present' in one image, showing the old and new side by side at Honeybourne on Tuesday, 2 August 2011. To the right, in this view towards Moreton-in-Marsh, the existing bi-directional line is now accompanied by installation of track that will become part of the new up line as it leaves the station. A summation of the past layout and a look to the future, when the two track panels either side of the Long Marston turnout are joined and the turnout is removed. *John Stretton*

Project successfully completed! Limited Edition

The COTSWOLD LINE Worcester to Oxford

This second section, prepared especially for those who have subscribed to the hardback publication, is dedicated by way of a tribute to those individuals who have conceived, designed and led the re-doubling project, and of course to those who have worked hard playing their part on the numerous worksites, culminating in the final completion of the Re-doubling Project in 2011. Every person involved in this project has played their part in all kinds of ways, from the 'men and their machines' out on site in all weathers, to the designers, the engineers, the individual project teams and the financial controllers plus a whole host of others. Without the dedicated hard work of everyone that this project has touched, we would not now be able to enjoy the benefits of this significantly enhanced section of line; and in acknowledging the inconvenience and disruption to rail passengers during the various periods of engineering work, your authors are convinced that the users of the Cotswold Line will find it massively improved, compared with what has gone before.

In producing this Subscribers Special Edition, both of us have derived much pleasure in our endeavours and great satisfaction in seeing the progress over time, which is reflected in the images that we have recorded along the way. We herewith present a random selection of these – plus one or two extras from John Whitehouse and Steve Widdowson, who assisted with the production of the original paperback – and ask our readers' forbearance at the lack of straightforward 'past & present' views in this section. In addition to the comparative 'before and after' views, we also felt it important to show various stages of the engineering works that were undertaken throughout much of 2011

and to which so many have contributed. We hope you will agree. We make no apology for concentrating on the work that came after the paperback book was completed and particularly for majoring on the section of line between Evesham and Moreton-in-Marsh, as it is those two places and locations in-between that have seen the majority of the most recent changes. We still make our journey from Worcester to Oxford, but in slightly different style. We are also pleased to include a number of views of the Vintage Trains' special charter train on 17 September 2011 over the Cotswold Line, which was organised to celebrate the achievements of the Project. It was good to see steam return to the route and we hope the reader will enjoy our selection of views.

Finally, it has to be said that without the assistance and encouragement from the staff of Network Rail, First Great Western, Amey Colas and Amey, our task would have been so much harder. The willingness and eagerness of project staff at all levels to co-operate has been outstanding and especially gratifying to your two authors. To all who have come across our respective paths, we say a huge 'thank you'. Deep down we feel we all enjoy a little 'wallowing in nostalgia' from time to time, and we hope this volume also satisfies that need. The images have been carefully chosen and we hope you enjoy them. If you would like to pass on any messages and/or comments about the collection, we would be pleased to hear them via the publisher. Thank you.

John Stretton & Tim Maddocks
October 2011

ASCOTT-UNDER-WYCHWOOD: Early on the morning of Monday 6 June 2011, David Northey of Network Rail cuts the Opening Day ribbon at Ascott-under-Wychwood. The first of the two major blockades of 2011 was given up by the engineers at 0400 hrs that morning, allowing trains to run over a double line of railway between Ascott and Charlbury for the first time since 1971. The brand new 71 metre-long Up platform can be seen in the background, in this view looking towards Charlbury and Oxford. The signalbox is behind the photographer at this point, on the Down side of the line. *John Stretton*

Introduction by Patrick Hallgate, Route Managing Director, Network Rail, Western Route

Since the publication of the paperback edition of this book, 'Devolution' has arrived on the Western Route of Network Rail as of 14 November 2011, together with all the benefits that this offers us all for the future. For me, as the new Route Managing Director, Western, the commissioning of the Cotswolds Redoubling Project in August 2011 illustrates very well the fact that I believe that the Western has the most exciting future of all the Network Rail Routes – with electrification, resignalling, CrossRail and Reading Remodelling, we will be the biggest building site in Europe for the next eight or nine years! The challenges of operating the railway in this environment are huge, but with a great team we will succeed not only in building a fantastic railway for the future but also in operating a high-performing railway right now. The restoration of double track for a significant portion of the Cotswold Line will make an important contribution to keeping the railway into London Paddington running on time during this period and beyond, and together with other projects to improve stations and rolling stock will offer customers clear improvements in the quality of their journeys. I am delighted to be able to make this contribution to the Subscribers Special Edition of *The Cotswold Line,* which will enable all those involved in this excellent project the opportunity to look back in future years and say, 'I helped build that!'

HONEYBOURNE: This is a sign that says it all, on 9 August 2011, just a few days into the second of the 2011 major blockades, a reflection of the major investment in the OWW route and indicative that the major works carried out by Network Rail will soon be coming to a conclusion. *John Stretton*

WORCESTER: As before, our new journey begins at Worcester, where No 5043 *Earl of Mount Edgcumbe* glides into Shrub Hill station at 0820 hrs on Saturday, 17 September 2011, on the outward leg of the 'Cathedrals Express' Tyseley-Paddington charter train. This was operated by Vintage Trains, based in Tyseley, to celebrate the completion of the re-doubling project and was the first steam charter train over the OWW route for many years. The train was very well patronised and together with Vintage Trains' other customers, First Great Western had booked a complete carriage to convey VIPs and other invited dignitaries in style over the refurbished route. *John Stretton*

Above **WORCESTER: A** busy scene at the east end of Shrub Hill on a summer Sunday in 1982, as an un-refurbished Class 50 eases into the station with a London Paddington to Hereford service (possible the 16.10?). Beyond the signal box on the right is the gabled frontage of the ex-Midland railway Goods Shed, which is still standing today, albeit no longer in railway use. On the left is a raft of engineer's wagons, quite possibly of the 'Grampus' type, standing in one of the through roads known locally as the 'Hereford Sidings'. These sidings are part of the ex-Great Western goods yard which is positioned out of picture behind the station. It is good to note that the array of lower quadrant signals survives to the present day, although the signalbox has acquired **UPVC** double glazed windows since this picture was taken. *Steve Widdowson*

Above right **WORCESTER:** Standing in 'Back Road Siding' behind platforms 2 & 3 at Worcester Shrub Hill, which was one of three roads specifically converted for HST stabling in 2010, No 43098 stands at the head of the HST rake that awaits its next call of duty, on Saturday 17 September 2011. The three sidings immediately beyond the HST form the 'Hereford Sidings', with further DB Schenker sidings and the Through Goods Lines in the background. *John Stretton*

Right **WORCESTER:** Taking water, No 5043 *Earl of Mount Edgcumbe* stands at Worcester on 17 September 2011, with the Vintage Trains' 'Cathedrals Express' bound for Paddington. A London Midland Class 150 'Sprinter' unit is stabled on the middle road in the background. The steam charter was not booked to take on water at Shrub Hill, but a navigational error by the road tanker driver led to him not being able to rendezvous with the train at the booked water stop at Droitwich. As a result, some two thousand gallons of water were hurriedly taken on at Worcester, less than half of what was required to fill the four and a half thousand gallon Hawksworth tender. This led to one of your authors (TM) making a hurried call to the driver of the road tanker and giving him directions to the signalbox yard at **Evesham!** *John Stretton*

GISHBORN CROSSING: This was the scene at Gishborn Crossing, approximately one mile west of Evesham on Thursday 18 August 2011, with just under four days left until the two week August blockade was due to be handed back. This view is looking west (towards Worcester), and shows the new double-to-single connection installed during this blockade. The red notice reads 'STOP, check points are correctly set before proceeding' and is a reminder to drivers of engineering trains and other on-track plant working in an Engineers Worksite to check the lie of the points before passing over them. Two Amey staff are hard at work, part of a larger gang that was working behind the photographer. Note the rail clamps in the foreground on both lines. These act in a similar way to conventional fishplates, albeit using two plates to clamp the rails together as a temporary measure, pending welding and stressing. A ballast train has visited this location, but further tamping would be done to improve the alignment before it was opened to passenger and freight services on 22 August 2011. *Tim Maddocks*

GISHBORN CROSSING:
Turning 180 degrees to the previous shot, we are now looking back towards Evesham, with the double track clearly evident. The gang of Amey staff continue to work on the new infrastructure. Gishborn Crossing is what is known as a 'User Worked Crossing' in modern railway parlance, but would previously have been known as a farm or occupation crossing. In this view, the crossing surface had been removed to facilitate the relaying of the track and would be restored shortly before the blockade was given up. *Tim Maddocks*

EVESHAM: On an unspecified date in early 1994, a pair of 'Dutch' civil engineers liveried Class 31s double head a train of spoil and scrap materials from Bescot in open wagons past Evesham signalbox, heading towards the civil engineers' tip at Honeybourne. The area around the signalbox appears completely undeveloped, although this would change within a few years, with a superstore being built only a few yards to the rear of the box. *Steve Widdowson*

EVESHAM: The slightly wider angle taken on 21 June 1996, shows industrial units appearing opposite the signalbox, on the course of the old Midland line to Ashchurch. 166208 is departing with a service towards Worcester. *Steve Widdowson*

EVESHAM: We now jump ahead to Friday 19 August 2011, just a few days away from the end of the final redoubling blockade and evidence of further development, both on and off the railway, is clear. A road-rail machine is working on the new Down line opposite the signalbox and various engineering staff clad in high-visibility orange are evident on site. The old Up Home signal structure still stands, albeit with the semaphore arm removed, and the new Down Starter colour light signal can be seen adjacent to it. Part of the redoubling scheme involved the removal of the two Down sidings at Evesham, and redundant track panels from the main line relaying can be seen stacked on the formation of one of those former sidings. New generator and relay rooms can be seen in the background behind the track panels. *John Stretton*

EVESHAM: The back of TM's head can be seen here, as he looks out to check that the road tanker driver has heeded his instructions, as the 'Cathedrals Express' arrives at Evesham to top up with water on Saturday 17 September 2011. A few minutes later the watering would be completed and the train pulled forward into the station to allow further passengers to board. *John Stretton*

EVESHAM: On a damp Thursday 18 August 2011, the photographer is standing on the now-disconnected and closed Down siding immediately to the west of Evesham signal box, looking east towards the station. The bracket carrying the former E32 Down Inner Home signal stands silhouetted against the overcast sky, whilst the rear of the new colour light turn-back signal E2453 can be seen immediately behind. This signal allows Up trains that have terminated in the Up platform at Evesham to be signalled back towards Worcester, without the need to introduce Pilotworking or Special Instructions and will be of considerable use during future engineering works or other occasions when train working needs to be amended. The two week August blockade is still in force, as evidenced by the road-rail machine standing in the Down platform, prior to recommencing work on the Down line outside the signal box. *Tim Maddocks*

LITTLETON & BADSEY: As the sign states, this is Littleton & Badsey level crossing, located at 104miles 31chains from Paddington, looking west towards Worcester, as seen on 10 October 2010. The level crossing surface and associated equipment, including lifting barriers etc., had only been renewed in a weekend blockade a few days earlier. The space for the new second line can clearly be seen between the newly-positioned lifting barriers. The station platforms used to stand at this point, with the ramps ending at the road level crossing, which takes the road linking the villages of Littleton and Badsey. *John Stretton*

LITTLETON & BADSEY: From the same viewpoint nearly a year later on 3 October 2011, the difference is obvious. The new down line is now in place and in use and the associated vegetation clearance has revealed the remains of the old down platform, still extant even though the station itself closed on 3 January 1966. The former concrete hut on the downside approach to the level crossing has also been removed. The very tall lighting and CCTV posts are prominent in both photographs, the level crossing being supervised and operated from Evesham signal box. *John Stretton*

CLAYFIELD CROSSING: is located about ¾-mile to the east of Littleton & Badsey, but is an automatic half barrier (AHB) type, owing to the lower status of the public road and less attendant traffic usage. This was the view on 10 October 2010 looking east in the Up direction towards Honeybourne, with the former crossing keepers cottage on the left. New troughing components are laid out on the opposite side of the line, as the existing troughing route in the foreground would have to be removed to accommodate the new Up line a few months later. *John Stretton*

CLAYFIELD CROSSING: The last major piece of the Cotswold Re-doubling Project to be completed was Clayfield Level Crossing, which for technical reasons remained closed to road traffic until some time after the completion of the main August 2011 blockade, an extended road closure having been agreed with the Local Authority. This is the view on 3 October 2011, with a nearby sign informing locals that the crossing would reopen on 7 October 2011. A brand new fence separates the new Up line from the cottage and its garden, as No 166213 speeds east with 1P40, the 0954 Great Malvern to Paddington service (See also, for comparison, the picture on page 45). *John Stretton*

HONEYBOURNE: This is the new junction for the Long Marston branch, now re-located to the west of Honeybourne station, as seen during the first week of the August blockade, on 11 August 2011. The yellow box of one of the clamp lock drives, together with the rodding of the 'back drive' in the 'four foot' can clearly be seen, as a S&T gang working for Amey make ready to move a new section of cable. The sleepers have been laid on the bottom ballast and the site is clearly awaiting the attentions of another ballast drop and tamping. There is a trailing crossover between the Up and Down lines immediately behind the photographer. This new junction, which is now controlled from the new mini-panel in Evesham signal box, is now designated 'Honeybourne Stratford Line Junction'. *Tim Maddocks*

HONEYBOURNE: In the very last days of the August 2011 blockade, engineering train 6W95 consisting of No 66130 hauling a rake of 20 Autoballasters is seen on the Down line just to the west of Honeybourne station on Friday, 19 August 2011. The new Up line is alongside; and the re-opened Up Yard is immediately the other side of the low bank and behind the new grey equipment cabinet. One end of the new trailing crossover can be seen in the Up line to the left of the locomotive. *John Stretton*

HONEYBOURNE: This Honeybourne Up
Yard on 9 April 2011, looking west towards
the site of the erstwhile buffer stops. The last
three remaining sidings had been disused
since B.R. days and had become completely
weed-choked in later years. The site had been
completely cleared back to bare earth by the
time this photo was taken, and track panels
lifted from other locations on the OWW line
were stacked in the yard area, prior to being
re-laid. The Up Yard initially consisted of three
parallel sidings prior to the 1920s, plus one
further siding of greater length between the
yard and the Up Main line. In 1923 the three
northern-most sidings in the Up yard were
lengthened to accommodate a total of 40
wagons each and another three of similar
length provided immediately to the north
of these. The official reason quoted for this
expansion of the Up Yard was to enable
the railway to manage an increase in local
fruit traffic, although it seems clear that the
sidings were used for other freight traffic
as well. A new head shunt was provided at
the same time, which ran in an easterly
direction behind the Up Relief platform
at Honeybourne station. Three new Down
sidings were provided to the south of the
station at the same time, these constituting
the 'Down Yard'.

HONEYBOURNE: We re-visit the Up Yard
on Sunday 14 August 2011 and can view progress from a slightly different angle. All three new
sidings have now been laid in and ballasted and a tamper is resting between shifts on the main
line in the background. Further tamping of the new sidings will be undertaken before they
are opened to normal traffic. This area formed one of the main site compounds and signing-
in points in the August 2011 blockade, with a large collection of portable offices and messing
facilities just out of view to the right.

HONEYBOURNE: On Friday, 19 August
2011, work is being progressed by Amey
Colas on the third siding in the Up Yard
with a Hydrex road/rail machine in
employment. Re-cycled concrete sleepers
have been laid out in the foreground,
awaiting the installation of second-hand
flat bottom rail, also recovered from
elsewhere on the OWW main line.
Honeybourne station is out of view, hidden
behind the pile of redundant track to the
right of the road/rail machine, although
the new station footbridge can be
discerned in the distance. *All John Stretton*

HONEYBOURNE:
A further view of
Honeybourne Up Yard
taken on 9 August 2011.
One of the new sidings
can be seen on the left of
the picture, with a new
set of points marking the
entrance to sidings 2 and
3 on the right. The line
of rails in the immediate
foreground is one of the
former redundant sidings
and would eventually
be recovered. A ground
position light controlling
the exit from the right hand
siding can also be seen.
This signal, together with
all other signals and points
at Honeybourne, are now
controlled from Evesham
signal box. *John Stretton*

HONEYBOURNE: The modern equivalent of the chain gang is seen just to the west of
Honeybourne station on 11 August 2011. These staff are working for Amey and are in the
process of moving lengths of new cable to the station area for installation and connection. Long
lengths of cable such as this are heavy and call for careful and coordinated handling! The Up and
Down Main lines are in the background, nearest to the 'chain gang', with the new connection to
the Long Marston line in the foreground. *Tim Maddocks*

HONEYBOURNE: Honeybourne station is seen on 9 April 2011, with the original former island platform prominent in this view looking west towards Worcester. The site of the Up Yard, already cleared of its old track and vegetation growth, can be seen in the distant background. The rusty track behind the island platform used to be the Up Relief platform line, but was latterly used as a connecting line to the Up Yard. It was subsequently to be lifted and re-laid as the new running line to Long Marston.

HONEYBOURNE: This is a similar view to the previous photograph, looking from the main road embankment over towards the Downside of the station on 9 August 2011. Concrete bases have already been constructed for the new station footbridge, and one of the new landings has already been lifted into position by the massive Baldwin's road crane. A further segment waits its turn on the lorry in the foreground, whilst the crane itself is lowering one of the Up side support columns into place.

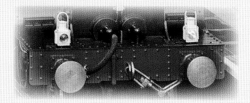

HONEYBOURNE: A short while later on the same day, the crane is now in the process of lifting the opposite landing into position on the Up side. Specialists from the bridge manufacturer keep a close watch on the fitment of the new steelwork. Note the new Up Main line in the foreground, already laid in place early during the August 2011 blockade, but still awaiting ballasting and tamping. *All John Stretton*

HONEYBOURNE: Once the two landings either side of the running lines had been fitted to their respective supports, it was then possible to crane the main span of the new station footbridge into position and the articulated lorry has moved into position on the main road overbridge, prior to the lifting straps being attached. In the foreground, work on the new Up platform has been progressing, with new copers, tactile paviours and a sub-base

of tarmac already installed. The black metal posts on the left will eventually support a new set of steel railings. Lighting columns and a new shelter in **FGW** corporate colours have also been erected. The old island platform structure did not conform to modern standards, so most of what you see in this photo is completely new, including the main platform support wall adjacent to the Up Main line. The Down line has been temporarily fenced off to provide a safe working area for those engaged on drainage and related works on the Down platform; this site will also be protected by worksite marker boards in the four foot of the running lines, which are out of view in this shot.

HONEYBOURNE: At precisely 1347 on Tuesday, 9 August 2011, the main span of the new footbridge at Honeybourne is gently lowered into place, to create a link between the two platforms for the first time for forty years. It is pleasing to note that Network Rail and First Great Western agreed that this (and also the new footbridge at Charlbury) should be ordered in the 'Light and Dark Stone' colours of the old Great Western Railway, colours which are now apparently available from a paint supplier's catalogue! *Both John Stretton*

HONEYBOURNE: Progress on the island platform on Sunday, 14 August 2011, as the northern end of the new footbridge awaits its DDA-compliant ramps to sit on the pillars on the platform. On the far right of the photo is the new line for traffic to/from Long Marston, alongside a redundant length of track showing where the GWSR will eventually be given access to the island platform. The re-instated Up Yard at this location, is in the right distance, housing a tamper and a trio of road/rail machines on this date. Note that the new Up Main line has now received a visit from a ballast train.

HONEYBOURNE: The main span of the new station footbridge is seen in place on 14 August 2011, whilst masonry work continues under the Up side supports, as part of construction work for the new pedestrian access ramps. It is apparent from this photograph that the two platforms are partially off-set, although the new Up platform is in fact longer than the existing Down side one. The new footbridge was built in Nottingham by **Brittons.** *Both John Stretton*

HONEYBOURNE: This view taken from the main road over bridge shows the area immediately to the east of Honeybourne station during relaying works on 9 August 2011. The former junction points in what will soon be the Down Main line have been left in place for now, albeit much cut back, to enable the relaying gangs to install the concrete sleepers and flat bottom rail of the new Up line. The redundant points would be removed and replaced with new plain line prior to the hand back of the blockade on 22 August, but were left in for a few days to facilitate the movement of engineers' trains and on-track plant. To the left of the photo is the new connection to the Long Marston line, with a portion of new, ballasted track already laid, together with a section of new steel sleepers awaiting their rails just beyond. In the distance the rear of an engineers train can be seen as it stands waiting further orders from the Engineering Supervisor. The Long Marston line can just be seen diverging to the left adjacent to the

rear of the train, this being the site of the former Honeybourne North Loop Junction, which used to have its own signal box. The last remaining signal box at Honeybourne on the OWW main line – Station South Signal Box – formerly stood on the down side approximately half way between the rear of the engineers train and the Hydrex machine on the right hand side.

HONEYBOURNE: Our photographer has moved position and we can now see the bridge from which the previous photograph was taken. This telephoto shot shows off well the precision with which Amey Colas have positioned the new concrete sleepers for the Up line. One of the new rails for said Up line lies across the redundant point on the left hand side, waiting to be 'thimbled' into position. The steel girder portion of the overbridge in the background dates from 1908, when Honeybourne station was substantially rebuilt to accommodate the significantly increased traffic resulting from the opening of the Cheltenham to Stratford main line.

HONEYBOURNE: We now get a closer look at the former relief line platform area, which will now accommodate the Long Marston line on the right hand side, and the future anticipated extension of the Gloucestershire & Warwickshire Steam Railway from Broadway on the left hand side. This would involve the reconstruction of the northern face of the former island platform and associated facilities by the steam railway. *All John Stretton*

1971 – 2011
40 YEARS ON
BACK ON
DOUBLE TRACK

2

Honeybourne celebrates!

Captions overleaf...

Previous page...

HONEYBOURNE NEW PLATFORM OPENING DAY

Inset top left **An historic moment on the opening day
after the completion of the final Cotswolds redoubling
blockade! At precisely 0600 on Monday, 22 August 2011,
as daylight made its first tentative appearance, No
43098 heads the very first passenger train into the new
Platform 2 at Honeybourne with a non-stop up working,
thus becoming the first HST set to ever grace this
alignment. When the previous up platform was removed
40 years earlier, the introduction of the prototype HST
was still some four years away. The new station facilities
are now installed, including a new GWR-style platform
bench donated by the Cotswold Line Promotion Group.**

Main picture **A large crowd of dignitaries and guests
congregate on the new station on the opening day of
the new facilities, 22 August 2011. The scale of the new
DDA-compliant footbridge is now apparent, although
a set of steps is also provided for the able-bodied who
wish to directly access the London-end of the platform.
The 'Light & Dark Stone' of the footbridge, together
with the Cotswold stone facing of the new platform
structure make for a pleasing combination! The length
of the new platform at Honeybourne is 140 metres,
which is long enough for most variations of Turbo units.
HSTs operated by First Great Western are all fitted
with Selective Door Opening (SDO), which allows the
Train Manager to select which doors are unlocked for
passenger use and thus enables the train to stop at
platforms which are shorter than the train itself. The
use of SDO also enabled a decision to be made to leave
the existing Down platform at its current length of 81
metres for the time being.**

Inset top right, right **For the early birds arriving at
Honeybourne station on the first day of re-opening -
22 August 2011 - 'breakfast' was provided free of charge
by Network Rail, who had secured the services of a local
catering company. One customer is about to receive
her goodies at precisely 0808 hrs. The contractors had
clearly not quite finished work in the car park, although
visitors' cars were still being accommodated in a
temporary car park in an adjacent field at the time.**

Inset top right, lower **The celebratory cake unveiled at
Honeybourne on Monday, 22 August 2011.**

Inset top right, left **Celebrating the culmination of the
Cotswolds Re-doubling Project, David Northey (left
– Commercial Scheme Sponsor for Network Rail)
and John Ellis (Chairman, CLPG) share a joke as they
cut the specially decorated cake at Honeybourne, on
Monday, 22 August 2011.** *All John Stretton*

SPOT THE AUTHOR ABOARD!

HONEYBOURNE: An historic moment on Saturday 17 September 2011 as 5043 'Earl of Mount Edgcumbe' thunders through Honeybourne station, heading the 'Cathedrals Express' from Tyseley to London Paddington. This charter train was operated by West Coast Railways on behalf of Vintage Trains and conveyed a mixture of fare-paying charter train passengers and VIPs and other guests specially invited by FGW, who had reserved an entire coach in the formation to celebrate the conclusion of the redoubling project. Despite the recent rain and the certainty of more wet weather to come from that leaden sky, several local enthusiasts have turned out to witness the first steam-hauled train to pass through Platform 2 at Honeybourne for over 40 years. *Jack Boskett*

Main picture **CAMPDEN TUNNEL:** The new lighting provided inside Campden Tunnel can be seen to good effect in this view looking west on 3 October 2011. Safety refuges can be seen with their white markings at regular intervals receding into the tunnel and S&T work is on-going, as evidenced by the attention to the troughing route.

Opposite top to bottom **CAMPDEN TUNNEL:** Turning around 180 degrees, this is the view looking east from the tunnel portal on 3 October 2011. In contrasting this photo with similar views taken earlier in the redoubling project, it can be seen how effectively the vegetation has recovered from previous earthworks. The radio mast for the new GSM-R 'cab-to-shore' radio system can be seen in the distance. Modellers of the modern railway scene will no doubt appreciate the fact that these are constructed to a standardised design and can now be found all over the network.

CAMPDEN TUNNEL: The Oxford portal of the tunnel is seen on 3 October 2011, and compares favourably with the 1966 view at the top of page 68. Double track is restored and the whole scene looks neat, tidy and ready for the 21st century! The very beginning of Autumn can be seen on some of the vegetation and this location would no doubt look very colourful a few weeks later. The new Down line is nearest the camera, with the original post-1971 single lie now slewed back over to the Up formation.

CAMPDEN TUNNEL: We change our angle again, in order to compare the view from ground level on 3 October 2011 with the very similar 2009 vantage points on page 69. The fast-growing grass seed used in the 2009 blockade has certainly lived up to its promises!

CHIPPING CAMPDEN: Work is progressing well at Chipping Campden level crossing on 9 August 2011 in this view looking towards Oxford. Campden Tunnel is approximately half a mile in rear of the photographer. Although the original road surface has been removed to facilitate other works and as a precursor to it's replacement, new lifting barrier units and 'wig wag' lights have been installed and are in the process of being wired up and tested by Amey technicians. In common with some of the other level crossings that were being upgraded in August 2011, the public road at this point had been closed for the duration of the two-week blockade, in conjunction with the local authority. *John Stretton*

CHIPPING CAMPDEN: Moving forward in time to 3 October 2011, we can see that Chipping Campden level crossing is now complete and fully functional, with a brand new road surface and new fencing. A new equipment building stands in the left of the photograph. Chipping Campden was the location of the main project offices during the August 2011 blockade, when Network Rail and its contractors hired a complete suite of offices in a new industrial estate adjacent to the railway and just out of sight behind the trees in the centre of this view. *John Stretton*

BLOCKLEY: In glorious autumn sunshine, 43092 brings up the rear of the 0935 Paddington-Hereford service as it passes Blockley level crossing on Sunday 17 October 2010. The OWW line here is still single for the moment, but this would soon change as mid-week night possessions were taken between December 2010 and May 2011 to install the new second running line. New bricks are stacked high in the adjacent Northcot Brickworks.

BLOCKLEY: The same location, albeit taken from a few feet further back towards Oxford is very different during the first week of the August blockade on 9 August 2011, as the new Down line has been installed and has received some top ballast, although further tamping will be required before it can be opened to normal traffic. Note how the ballast has been cleared away where rail joints have been welded. Two of the new 'wig-wag' flashing light units have been installed and the concrete bases for the pair nearer the photographer await the installation of their posts. With the level crossing surface completely removed for trackwork and it's own renewal, it is only the presence of the embryonic new level crossing equipment that reminds us that there should be a crossing here at all!

BLOCKLEY: Following concentrated work earlier in the month, Blockley level crossing, to the west of Moreton-in-Marsh, now has a full set of barriers guarding the double track, protective railings, guard rails, and equipment room. Some 9 days after the end of the August 2011 commissioning blockade, 166214 speeds towards the crossing with 1P40, the 0954 Great Malvern-Paddington service on Wednesday, 31 August. Protective coatings on the rails through the level crossing are apparent in this view.
All John Stretton

MORETON-IN-MARSH:
A pair of Class 40's, Nos. 40057 & 40084, make an unusual sight at Moreton-in-Marsh on 8 May 1982, as they ease onto the then 11 mile double-track section to Ascott-under-Wychwood at the head of the SVR Railtours' 'Cotswold Venturer' charter train. This had originated at York earlier in the day and was heading for London Paddington. Whether this was the first visit of Class 40's to the route is debateable, but it can certainly be considered in the 'extremely rare' category at the very least! The train returned north via Kemble and the 'Golden Valley' route to Standish Junction. The former dairy buildings can be seen behind the locomotives.
John Whitehouse

MORETON-IN-MARSH: At long last the route north-westwards from Moreton-in-Marsh station is again graced with double track. The former double-to-single connection has recently been removed at the start of the August 2011 blockade and new sections of plain line installed to connect the respective sections of the Up and Down Main lines. On Tuesday, 9 August 2011 during the first week of the blockade, a Hydrex WX170 MegaRailer road/rail machine trundles away from the station towards Honeybourne. At this point in the blockade, Moreton-in-Marsh station was under the possession of the engineers and passenger services from Oxford were terminating at Charlbury, with bus connections conveying passengers forward along the line of the OWW route to Worcester and intermediate stations. This was mainly to enable the crossover at the south end of the station to be renewed, as this would be required for use by passenger trains during the second week, when the station reverted to operational use. The clean ballast of the new track contrasts with the older track through the station platforms, but measures were also in hand to clean up this area! MM5 signal, which formerly controlled access onto the old single line to Evesham, now guards the Down Main line towards the next running signals, which after the commissioning of this project are at Honeybourne. *John Stretton*

MORETON-IN-MARSH: Vigorous weed growth earlier in the year had been killed by the weed killing train some weeks previously, but in order to improve the appearance of the infrastructure through Moreton-in-Marsh station, clearance work was arranged during the first week of the August blockade to remove the vegetation and generally clear up the tracks between the platforms. Here we see a gang of sub-contractors  under the supervision of an Amey foreman clearing weeds from the Up main line outside the signalbox. The line was under possession at this point of the blockade, with passenger trains from Oxford terminating at Charlbury. *Tim Maddocks*

MORETON-IN-MARSH: Changes to the track layout and signalling at Moreton-in-Marsh during the first week of the August blockade required much concentrated work by the team of Network Rail locking fitters to the equipment underneath the box and one of your authors was afforded a rare opportunity to photograph the conversion work on Tuesday, 9 August 2011. *John Stretton*

MORETON-IN-MARSH: On 10 August 2011 the Network Rail Maintenance Projects team are hard at work renewing the main-to-main crossover at the south end of Moreton-in-Marsh station. The disc cutter in the foreground has been left on the Up main line and the new bottom ballast covering the empty space of the crossover has nearly been fully compacted. The road-rail machine in the centre right of the photo is getting ready to start lifting the first of the new bullhead point track panels into position. The former Up siding has now been disconnected and the place formerly occupied by 22B points just before the over bridge will soon be taken up with plain line. Redundant track panels are stacked over on the site of the former Down Siding and a DB Schenker Class 66 loco forms one end of a 'top and tailed' engineers train standing on the Up main line just beyond the bridge. *Tim Maddocks*

MORETON-IN-MARSH: Moreton-in-Marsh's new semaphore signal MM27 is seen to good effect on Friday 19 August 2011, as 43031 brings up the rear of the departing 1451 service to London Paddington. During the second week of the August 2011 blockade Moreton acted as a temporary terminus for services from London and Oxford. The inward working of this set had terminated in the Down platform and is seen passing through the re-laid main-to-main crossover. *John Stretton*

MORETON-IN-MARSH: The Cotswolds Redoubling Project has resulted in all signals along the line of route being changed to LED colour lights, with the exception of the area controlled by the one remaining mechanical frame at Moreton-in-Marsh, which remains an 'island' of semaphore signals. One of the new facilities provided at Moreton by the Project was a new Up-direction 'turn back' signal on the Down line. This enables Down trains to terminate in the Down platform and simply return towards Oxford via the re-laid main-to-main crossover as a fully interlocked and signalled move. This is the new MM27 signal, which now controls these moves, a facility which will be very useful during any future engineering works or other perturbations to the train service. Prior to the August 2011 blockade, any passenger train wishing to make this move would either have to make a complicated shunt to the Up platform or would require special authority. The existing shunt signal MM20 is retained at the foot of the new signal. Due to manufacturing issues, the new signal structure for MM27 wasn't available, so the project team have sensibly re-cycled a redundant signal from Evesham, which is seen in position on Sunday 14 August 2011 and ready for the resumption of passenger services the following day. *John Stretton*

MORETON-IN-MARSH: Another photo taken by one of your authors of the other, as John Stretton hurries to the front of the 'Cathedrals Express' on Saturday 17 September 2011 to get a decent shot of 'Earl of Mount Edgcumbe!' Other folk have already gathered around the locomotive, including a couple of reporters, who are interviewing a VIP guest on the footplate. *Tim Maddocks*

MORETON-IN-MARSH: The identity of the VIP guest is revealed as the Rt. Hon. Theresa Villiers MP, Minister for Transport, who was a guest of First Great Western on the 'Cathedrals Express' on 17 September 2011. Here she is seen with Vintage Trains' Chief Engineer Bob Meanley in the cab of 5043 'Earl of Mount Edgcumbe' prior to departure from Moreton-in-Marsh. A cab permit had been arranged for the Minister, who rode on the locomotive through to Charlbury. *John Stretton*

MORETON-IN-MARSH: A less desirable aspect of major engineering works, perhaps, but nonetheless sometimes unavoidable is the use of road transport in lieu of trains to maintain a service for customers. This is the scene outside Moreton-in-Marsh station on Friday, 19 August 2011 as a pair of coaches wait for passengers off the 1421 arrival from Paddington to board. They will then be conveyed onward to stations to Worcester. *John Stretton*

MORETON-IN-MARSH: A rare steam working over the Cotswolds line occurred on 19 November 1994, when the Severn Valley railway-based pairing of Ivatt Mogul No. 46521 and BR Standard 2-6-4 Tank No. 80079 worked the Derby to London Paddington leg of Flying Scotsman Services' 'Capital Envoy' railtour from Worcester Shrub Hill. The train is seen standing in Moreton in the Marsh after taking water prior to continuing south to the Capital. It is interesting that even as recently as 1994 such obvious trespass by enthusiasts and local people was tolerated, whereas improved fencing and lineside safety rules today would mean that such scenes are no longer considered acceptable. *John Whitehouse*

ASCOTT-UNDER-WYCHWOOD: On 31 May 2011 during the first Cotswolds blockade of that year a small gang of Amey Colas PW staff at Ascott-under-Wychwood discuss the next item of work for the road rail machine standing on the Up line behind them in a brief moment of sunshine after heavy rain. Note the engineering train in the old EWS colours standing adjacent to them on the Down line. *John Stretton*

ASCOTT-UNDER-WYCHWOOD: On the same date, the photographer turned 180 degrees to give us the view looking east towards Oxford. The level crossing surface has been removed to facilitate the installation of new track and would later be replaced with a much improved road surface and new barrier equipment, the public road remaining closed in accordance with a local authority Road Closure Notice for the duration of the works. Whilst all this was going on, the signaller was not left to have a 'quiet life', because the old mechanical signalling lever frame was dismantled inside the signal box and a new signalling control panel installed. One can only hope that he was left with an electrical supply to keep the kettle boiling! *John Stretton*

CHARLBURY: On 14 October 2011, Prime Minister David Cameron unveiled a plaque at Charlbury station that read, in part, to "...celebrate station investment and service improvements along the North Cotswold Line", following the recent Doubling Project. Lord Faulkner of Worcester speaks to welcome the PM, who is flanked by Mark Hopwood, FGW MD and First Group CEO Tim O'Toole (extreme right).*FGW*

OXFORD: We end this celebration of the Cotswolds Redoubling Project with this magnificent view of No 5043 *Earl of Mount Edgcumbe* on 17 September 2011 appropriately enough at Oxford, as she takes water in the loop to the south of the station, whilst working the Vintage Trains' 'Cathedrals Express' charter train to London Paddington. *Tim Maddocks*

List of Subscribers

Network Rail
First Great Western

Ade James
Adrian Bridges
Adrian Saunders
Alfie Russell
Allan Chapman
Andrew Pennington
Andrew V Lynham
Andrew Wilkins
Andrew Wilson
Andrew Youdell
Andy Coston
Andy Heather
Andy Jones
Andy Spencer
Andy Taylor
Andy Wilson
Angela Bradley

Barney Hodge
Barry Greening
Bob Bemand
Bob Meanley
Brett Hellyer
Brian Baralos
Brian Clayton
Brian Vaux
Bryan Keetch

Cath Whitelaw
Chris Aldridge
Chris Brock
Chris Howchin
Chris Prior
Christine Millard
Clive Jowett
Colin Field
Colin Flack
Colin Oakley
Craig Kinsey

D R Davidson
Danny Scroggins
Darren Fairley
Darren Robinson
Daryl Stephenson
Dave Pagett
Dave Skipsey
David Alyn Aspinall
David Balme
David Emms

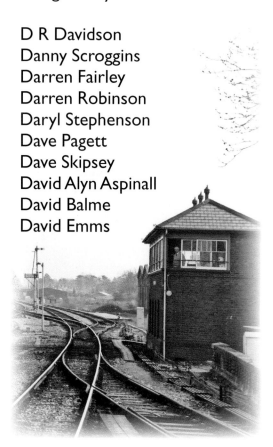

List of Subscribers

David Guy
David Hazell
David Humphrys
David Karabuha
David Mead
David Morton
David Northey
David Smith
David Tyler
David Wilson
Dean Brookes
Denise Johnson
Derek Potter
Don Church
Don Knight

Fraser Pithie

Garry Wilkinson
Gary Morris
Gary Watson
Gavin George
George Bryant
Gerry Kane
Gethin Jones
Glyn Maddocks
Graeme Christmas
Graham Bellamy
Graham Dargie
Graham Penfold
Graham Staddon
Graham Wells
Grahame Nash

List of Subscribers

Ian Baxter
Ian Cowley
Ian Finch
Ian Morton
Ian Murray
Ian Waggott
In memory of Ted Emery
Ivan Johnson
Ivor Sutton

Jack Boskett
James Carleton
James Garland
James O'Gorman
James Watts
Jamie Fabian
Jane Galbraith
Janet Baker
Janet Stevens
Jason Green

Jeremy Elkes
Jeremy Swift
Jo Sharpe
John Dora
John Dyer
John Farmer
John H Eales
John Harvey
John Jenkins
John Shipston
John Spencer Gilks
John Stamp
John Whitehouse
John Young
Jon Godden
Jonathan Kelway
Julian Crow
Julian Tansell
Julie Brown

List of Subscribers

Keith Barnes
Keith Farmer
Keith Gardner
Kelly Davis
Ken & Mary Edwards
Kevin Heywood &Tammy Stretton
Kevin Quigley
Kevin Simpson
Kevin Staddon

Lee Moyle
Lynn Earl

Malcolm Parsons
Mandy Reid

Marcus Kisiel
Margaret Powell
Maria Ivory
Mark Abbott
Mark Arrand
Mark Langman
Martin Duff
Martin Loader
Martin Smith
Martin Street
Martin Worsfold
Martyn Sanders
Martyn Tilford
Matthew Golton
Matthew Knight

List of Subscribers

Maurice Kerrigan
Mavis Choong
Michael Dart
Michael 'Doc' Doherty
Mickey Martin
Mike & Jo Horry
Mike Broom
Mike Brunt
Mike Franklin
Mike Gallop
Mike Obst
Mike Organ
Mike Romans
Mike Smith
Mike Tedstone
Mike Upton
Mike Ward
Morag Athersmith
Mr & Mrs I Vallance
Mr A Fletcher
Mr Bob & Jane Carr
Mr Brian Moore

Mr Chris Fry
Mr Gary Hale
Mr Stephen Amphlett
Mrs H A Bowyer

Neil Beckley
Neil Parr
Neville Bond
Nic Scott
Nicholas Jones LRPS
Nick Millington
Nick Tozer Railway Books
Nigel Rose
Nik Thomson

Oliver Evans
Oliver Lovell

Patrick Hallgate
Patrick Lawless
Patrick North
Paul Berwick
Paul Critchley

List of Subscribers

Paul Gardner
Paul Hayward
Paul Martin
Paul Richards
Paul Smith
Paul Stanford
Peter Day
Peter Langman
Peter Luff
Peter Muir
Peter Scurrell
Peter Trowbridge
Phil Stevens
Phillip Bellamy

Rachel Barnes
Rev A L P Slack
Rich Long
Richard Atkinson
Richard Burningham
Richard Cole
Richard Dugdale
Richard Eccles
Richard Moreton
Rob and Queenie Ridgway
Rob Emmons
Robert Robotham
Rod Cameron
Roger Hemming
Ross Mahoney
Russell Gange

S B Thomas
Sharon Michell
Shaun Mahy
Simon Ball
Simon Jacklin
Simon Spencer
Stephen Atkinson
Stephen F Heginbotham
Stephen Gilbert
Stephen Taylor
Stephen Widdowson
Steve Appleton
Steve Claridge
Steve Cole
Steve Elliott

List of Subscribers

Steve James
Steve Mathias
Steven Lewis
Stuart Firth
Stuart Hitch
Sue Yeo

Teresa Ceesay
The Revd Neil Hibbins
Thomas Ford
Tim Ingman
Tim Mayo
Tom Woodworth
Trevor Hodgson
Trevor Lambert Gorwyn

Vic Gackowski

William Crossley
William Mackinnon

Publisher's Dedication

The 'footplate crew' at Past & Present Publishing Ltd would like to place on record their appreciation of the enthusiasm and support that has been so much in evidence from Network Rail, First Great Western and all the many contractors throughout the preparation of this celebration volume. We also recognise and appreciate the valuable support of the Cotswold Line Promotion Group.

The redoubling of the Cotswold Line is an inspirational example and represents and reflects the true spirit and ongoing hard work, dedication and determination of all those who are working to build and develop Britain's reinvigorated railway of the future.

Index of locations

Captions for pages i-vii

Page i
In a view looking south towards Norton Junction, on 26 March 1993, the signalman at Worcester looks towards the photographer from his lofty vantage point. *Steve Widdowson*

Page ii
A previous incarnation of the celebratory steam special of the Doubling Project sees 'Castle Class' 4-6-0 No 5029 *Nunney Castle* passing the signalbox at Evesham, at the head of the return working of 'The Cathedrals Express' charter from Didcot to Worcester, on 27 June 1993. *Steve Widdowson*

Page iii
On a dull day, DMU set No B434 pauses at Kingham on 10 June 1982, with a Worcester-Oxford service. Note the very open feel at the station at this date. *John Acton/John Stretton collection*

Page iv
A pause in procedings at Honeybourne on 9 August 2011, as the main part of the new station footbridge is about to be lowered into position. *John Stretton*

Page v
Class 50 No 50007 *Hercules* (its original name) pauses at Charlbury with an up express, 15 May 1982. *John Whitehouse*

Page vi
Kevin Connolly and sound recordist interview the celebrities on the footplate of 'Castle Class' 4-6-0 No 5043 *Earl of Mount Edgcumbe*, at Moreton-in-Marsh on 17 September 2011, during the special steam run from Worcester to Paddington. *Tim Maddocks*

Page vii and author signature page
'Castle Class' 4-6-0 No 5043's 'hot box' with traditional enamel tea containers on 17 September 2011. *Tim Maddocks*

Major work in progress at Ascott-under Wychwood on 31 May 2011 (see page 159). *John Stretton*